# AFTER SEXUAL TRAUMA

## FINDING RENEWAL IN CHRIST

Camille Cates

New Growth Press, Greensboro, NC 27401
newgrowthpress.com


Cover Design: Studio Gearbox, studiogearbox.com
Interior Typesetting/eBook: Lisa Parnell, lparnellbookservices.com

ISBN: 978-1-64507-561-5 (paperback)
ISBN: 978-1-64507-562-2 (ebook)

Library of Congress Cataloging-in-Publication Data on file

Printed in Colombia

29 28 27 26 25 1 2 3 4 5

"Camille Cates compassionately, vulnerably, and lovingly helps the person who has experienced sexual assault know the love, care, and life of Christ. This deeply honest book speaks into the struggles and questions people have, bringing wise, loving and biblical hope and life."

**Anne Dryburgh,** Author; counselor; coordinator, Biblical Counseling Coalition European Network

"This book is a compassionate, biblically grounded guide for healing from sexual trauma. Weaving personal experience with Scripture, Camille Cates affirms victims' innocence and points to Christ's redemptive hope. It's a vital resource for counselors and survivors, upholding biblical counseling's commitment to truth, care, and restoration."

**Julie Ganschow,** Founder, Reigning Grace Counseling Center, Kansas City, MO; certified biblical counselor

"Camille bravely addresses the deep pain of sexual abuse, offering hope and healing through Christ. With compassion and clarity, she connects the realities of sexual trauma to the redemptive power of the gospel. This book doesn't shy away from hard truths but leads readers toward restoration and redemption in Jesus."

**Liz Beck,** Founder, Hope for Addiction; certified biblical counselor

"Camille offers tender truths grounded in Scripture to the deep wounds of sexual trauma with honesty, grace, truth, and hope. She compassionately affirms victims' dignity and helps them understand they are not forgotten, but cherished by El-roi, the God who sees, hears, and restores. Camille wants those suffering from sexual trauma to see themselves not as victims or survivors but overcomers!"

**Georgia Purdom,** VP of Educational Content, Answers in Genesis

"Whenever I read a book by Camille Cates, I am overwhelmed with the love of God and his plan for healing amid betrayal, helplessness, and disorienting suffering. In this book, you will be confronted with Camille's humble transparency about sexual trauma. But as God rebuilt Camille's ruins through the precious blood of Christ, so she teaches us the way of the Savior with his daughters. Camille leads readers to lay hold of the gospel's promises through the inerrant Word so that healing emerges and overcomers live in the freedom of Christ. This book is pure gospel gold and must be read by all Christians seeking to help restore lives after sexual trauma."

**Rosaria M. Butterfield,** Author of *The Secret Thoughts of an Unlikely Convert* and *Five Lies of Our Anti-Christian Age*

"*After Sexual Trauma* is a gift to survivors and those who walk beside them. With personal vulnerability, researched wisdom, and biblical fidelity, Camille Cates addresses the hard questions sexual trauma raises. She consistently points to the person and work of Christ, reminding us of the gospel's power to redeem and transform us in every affliction."

**Eric M. Schumacher,** Author of *The Good Gift of Weakness*

"Camille engages readers with the kind of candor and hope that only comes through lived experience. She draws both from her own painful past and years of counseling conversations with sexual trauma survivors. If you're looking for a book to help you process what's happened to you in a redemptive way, know that this resource is written by a compassionate and trustworthy guide."

**Christine M. Chappell,** Author of *Midnight Mercies*; *Hope + Help Podcast* host, IBCD; certified biblical counselor

"*After Sexual Trauma* overflows with hope, healing, compassion, and grace. If you feel broken, defiled, or beyond repair, this book gently reminds you that you are not. Camille writes with the tenderness of a trusted counselor and the steady voice of an advocate. Her words deeply helped me, and I'm confident they will help you too."

**Paul Tautges,** Pastor; counselor; author of *A Small Book for the Hurting Heart*

## DEDICATION

This book is dedicated to the women and men who have shared their stories of sexual trauma with me. For many, I was the first person you told, and I'm deeply grateful for your trust. Thank you for allowing me to walk alongside you as you found renewal in Christ and embraced the comfort and hope only he can provide. This book was written to honor the Lord and his amazing work in you and me with the belief that he will do the same in countless others. My prayer is that the seeds of our sorrows will bloom into shouts of joy in heaven.

*Those who plant in tears*
*will harvest with shouts of joy.*

*They weep as they go to plant their seed,*
*but they sing as they return with the harvest.*

Psalm 126:5–6 (NLT)

# CONTENTS

# INTRODUCTION

Helpless. Confused. In denial. That's how I felt after experiencing sexual assault. It happened against my will, beyond my control. I was powerless to overcome it alone. I wanted to pretend it didn't really happen—to bury it deep and lock it away. But denying it didn't erase it.

As time went on, the trauma that I had suppressed disoriented me and distorted my thinking. I wrestled with who I was, and I didn't allow myself to wrestle out who God was amid my suffering. For several years, I ran from God, wandering in a spiritual wasteland—until my self-destructive path led me right back to him.

In the Bible, the story of Hagar is one of immense suffering. She was an Egyptian servant, brought into a foreign land where her sole purpose was to be at her mistress Sarai's beck and call. Her life was not her own. So, when Sarai—desperate after years of barrenness—devised a plan for her husband Abram to take Hagar as a second wife and conceive a child through her, Hagar had no say. She was used for someone else's gain, her body treated as a means to an end (Genesis 16:1–4).

Imagine Hagar's world for a moment. In that time and culture, she had no choice, no voice—only the expectation to obey. Her life was one of "Do as you're told." Eventually, she did become pregnant from this forced union, which, of course, caused friction between her and Sarai. That's when the abuse took another turn. First, she was used for someone else's gain, and then she was treated harshly, her value completely diminished. Rather than endure relentless abuse, Hagar chose to run away—into the wilderness.

Alone in the vast wilderness, Hagar had nowhere to go. She was far from her Egyptian homeland with no hope of returning. But it was in this desolate place that something extraordinary happened—God revealed himself to her. The angel of the Lord appeared to her and asked, "Where have you come from, and where are you going?" (Genesis 16:8). God wasn't asking about her geographical location. This was an invitation—an opportunity for Hagar to open her heart to him, to bring her confusion, pain, and fears to the One who knew all she had suffered. And she responded with raw honesty: "I'm running away from my mistress Sarai" (Genesis 16:8–10).

God didn't scold her or condemn her for running. Instead, he met her in her deepest anguish, with compassion, tenderness, and the promise of a son. God said, "You are to name him Ishmael (which means 'God hears'), for the Lord has heard your cry of distress" (Genesis 16:11). But God didn't just hear Hagar's cries; he saw her. Moreover, God revealed that he had a future planned for her—a future she could never have imagined possible. She would have more descendants than she could count (Genesis 16:10). Hagar would have a family of her own.

In that most vulnerable moment with God, Hagar did something remarkable—she gave God a name. She called him *El-roi*—the God who sees me (Genesis 16:13). For the first time, someone acknowledged her worth. Her Creator saw her in her pain, and in doing so, he gave her dignity, value, and the courage to face the future.

Hagar's encounter with God is a powerful reminder that no matter how deep your pain or how unseen you may feel, God does see you. And he sees what no one else does—the tears you shed in secret, the scars that linger in your heart and mind, the hidden battles you fight every day. He sees you, even in the spiritual wilderness you may be wandering through right now. But God doesn't just see your pain; he sees your future and wants to provide you with hope in the promise of a Son—his Son, Jesus.

When you look to Jesus, you meet with the One who knows you in your rawest, most fragile state. He sees every wound, every tear, every part of your story. He doesn't run from your pain. He enters it. He walks with you, offering comfort, understanding, and renewal in himself.

If you're unsure of who this God is—the God who sees you—I encourage you to keep reading. This journey toward healing and renewal after sexual trauma begins with seeking *El-roi*, the God who not only sees your past and present suffering but also holds your future. You are not unseen. You are not alone. Like Hagar, God sees you and is ready to meet you where you are—to comfort you, restore you, and lead you into the future he has planned for you.

# Chapter 1

# DID THAT REALLY JUST HAPPEN?

I was a freshman in high school when it happened.

He looked so cool as he walked down the crowded hallway at school. He was a couple of years older than me and wore confidence along with his sleek black leather jacket—I was enamored. As he passed by, our eyes met, and I felt my heart skip a beat. He flashed a grin, and I was completely undone. With his striking green eyes and olive complexion, I couldn't shake the feeling that I had to find a way for him to notice me. Thankfully, my friend Annie knew him. She had a crush on his best friend, and they talked all the time. Before long, we came up with a plan—we'd casually meet up with the guys at the movies.

Friday night finally came, and I dressed to impress, secretly hoping for a chance to hold hands and maybe even get my first kiss. My mom dropped off Annie and me at the theater, and as soon as she drove away, we walked right back out. We were meeting the guys in the parking lot. Sure enough, there they were, leaning against their motorcycles, the chrome gleaming under the streetlights. The excitement and thrill of the moment rushed over me. Everything felt so new, so exhilarating.

We chatted for a while, exchanging flirtatious banter. At one point, he put his arm around me, and before I knew it, he playfully scooped me up and threw me over his shoulder like it was nothing. He was tall and strong. I kicked and laughed, playfully yelling, "Put me down!" But he didn't set me down until he'd carried me off, around to the back of the building.

At first, I was relieved to be somewhere private. I didn't want my first kiss to happen in front of everyone—especially not in full view of peers from the local high schools who crowded the theater on Friday nights. That would've made me the center of Monday's gossip. Once he put me down and I was back on my feet, he leaned me against the building and moved in close to kiss me. It all felt exciting and incredible—until suddenly, it didn't.

What began as thrilling quickly turned into something that felt wrong and scary. His hands started going places I didn't want them to. "Hey, let's stop and go back. I need to get back to Annie," I pleaded. But before I knew it, he had put his hand down my jeans. I didn't know what to do at that moment. He put his whole body weight against me, making me even more uncomfortable as he gratified himself at my expense. I just froze until it was over.

Even though I was upset over what had happened, I was still captivated by his swagger and charm. I felt a confusing mix of emotions—unease over his sexual aggression, but also excitement at the thought of being his girlfriend. We held hands as we walked back to our friends. Then, with his arms firmly around my waist, he kissed my neck and cheek. The movie was ending soon, so Annie and I headed back inside. The night was over.

I don't remember much after that. I think I was in shock, asking myself, *Did that really just happen?* It all unfolded so quickly. At the time, I wasn't sure how to process it. Even though we hadn't had sex, I knew something had changed. I didn't feel quite so innocent anymore.

By Monday, I was eager to see him at school. In my mind, we were a couple now. But I had no idea I'd made an unexpected enemy. Another girl had a crush on him, and she despised me because he never gave her the time of day. As if that wasn't awkward enough, we shared the same desk. She sat there for biology in the morning, and I had the same seat during homeroom in the afternoon.

Later that week, to my complete horror and utter embarrassment, I sat down at my desk and saw something written across the corner of the laminated top. It wasn't a note addressed to me; it was about me. She had detailed everything my crush had done to me behind the movie theater, with the word "SLUT" written in all caps next to my name. Anyone who had previously sat at my desk would have read the cruel gossip this mean girl had spitefully scribbled before I could erase it with my pencil. I was mortified and furious. My innocence had been stolen, and yet I was being labeled with this derogatory term for women.

I was devastated. But it would be years before I realized that I had experienced sexual assault and how deeply it had affected my life. Looking back, the assault had a profound impact on my choice to be sexually promiscuous as a teen. It skewed my understanding of love, and I began seeking affection in exchange for sexual acts from subsequential romantic partners. This only piled on more guilt and shame.

That incident, along with the damage to my reputation at school, led me down a dark road. I devalued myself. I no longer believed I had worth or value before God or anyone else. At the time, I was a professing Christian, believing with all my heart that Jesus died on the cross for my sins. But after the assault, I felt buried under guilt and shame because of what I had endured.

In time, God brought a wonderful man into my life, using him to help me grow as a follower of Christ. He had just graduated from seminary and accepted a position as a youth pastor at a small church in West Texas, not far from our hometown. We married, and I moved there, eager to serve in ministry with him.

In that little West Texas town, there weren't many young couples our age. Most had gone away to college and moved on. For some reason, as a young couple without children, we attracted a great deal of attention from the congregants. Reflecting on those early years in ministry, I remember one unsettling incident that made me again question, *Did that really just happen?*

On Sundays, we often enjoyed church potlucks, which provided a wonderful opportunity for getting to know people and eating some fabulous homemade dishes. On one occasion, we sat at a table with a deacon and his family. As we shared stories, laughed together, and listened to them recount the church's history, we developed a friendly rapport.

As it was time to leave, we stood between the tightly arranged rows of tables and began to file out of the fellowship hall. Suddenly, I felt a squeeze on my behind and froze. A whirlwind of thoughts raced through my mind: *That couldn't be what I think it is. Right? Surely not?* I turned to see the man smiling nonchalantly, as if nothing had happened.

Later, I confided in my husband, who was at a loss for how to respond. We both tried to brush off the incident, feeling powerless to act due to our fear of potential repercussions from this deacon who had close ties to our pastor. As outsiders in this community, we worried that my husband might lose his first church job. We decided to try to avoid this man as much as possible to prevent a repeat of that uncomfortable situation—or worse. Ultimately, we left the church to serve elsewhere.

## QUESTIONING YOUR EXPERIENCE

It's natural to question whether you were sexually abused or assaulted, as confusion and doubt can often cloud your understanding of what transpired. Deuteronomy 22:25–27 offers a poignant perspective on this issue, providing both clarity and comfort. It establishes a theological framework that emphasizes the innocence of the one who has been wronged and holds the perpetrator personally accountable for their actions.

> But if the man encounters an engaged woman in the open country, and he seizes and rapes

> her, only the man who raped her must die. Do nothing to the young woman, because she is not guilty of an offense deserving death. This case is just like one in which a man attacks his neighbor and murders him. When he found her in the field, the engaged woman cried out, but there was no one to rescue her.

This passage from the Old Testament addresses the scenario of a woman being assaulted in a field, far from any help. What are the key points? First, there is the recognition of the victim's innocence; second, an understanding of her helplessness; and third, a clear condemnation of the assailant.

## RECOGNIZING INNOCENCE

Scripture emphatically declares in Deuteronomy 22:25, "But if the man encounters an engaged woman in the open country, and he seizes and rapes her, only the man who raped her must die." This powerful assertion affirms the victim's innocence. It affirms your innocence. It affirms mine. Often, those who have been sexually abused or assaulted grapple with feelings of guilt and self-blame, questioning their actions and wondering if they somehow invited or deserved the assault. However, this passage offers reassurance: They are blameless, and the responsibility for the sin and the guilt lay entirely with the perpetrator.

The comparison of assault to murder in this passage is significant. It states, "This case is just like one in which a man attacks his neighbor and murders him." God's deliberate analogy between rape and murder underscores the violence and violation inherent in sexual abuse and assault, emphasizing the victim's powerlessness in such situations. Just as a person who is attacked and murdered is helpless to prevent their death, a victim of sexual assault is similarly powerless to stop it. The phrase "in the field" symbolizes isolation and vulnerability, reinforcing the inability to escape or find assistance, and it does not indicate compliance or consent.

Deuteronomy 22:25 is clear-cut in its condemnation of the assailant: "Only the man who raped her must die." The severity of this Old Testament penalty reflects the gravity of the crime and places the culpability solely on the perpetrator. It leaves no room for doubt about who is at fault. Knowing God's law regarding cases of rape can help you understand that the perpetrator of your abuse is entirely responsible for the crime committed against you.

## OVERCOMING SELF-BLAME

When questioning whether you were sexually abused or assaulted, it is vital to combat feelings of self-blame. Anchor yourself to this biblical affirmation of your innocence as a foundational truth. Reflect on God's perspective of your suffering, and remember that being in a vulnerable situation did not mean you were complicit. Your actions—or lack thereof—during the incident did not justify what happened in any way.

Sexual assault or abuse often involves coercion, manipulation, or physical force, leading to a sense of helplessness like that experienced by the woman described in the biblical field. It can help to reflect on your own situation and recognize the power dynamics at play. Did a youth pastor persuade you to go to a room out of sight from the group under the pretense of "talking," only to grope you and then tell you not to say anything? Perhaps a boss asked you to stay late to work on a project. Even though you never consented to what happened in his office behind closed doors, you wrestle with feelings of guilt. Or maybe, as a child, an older cousin organized a "game" of playing doctor. He was physically stronger and threatened to make you look bad to the rest of the family if you didn't comply with his demands.

Recognizing that you were in a vulnerable position—whether isolated or overpowered—can help clarify the reality of your experience. This understanding begins to dismantle any deeply held belief that you could have done something differently to prevent what happened. Acknowledging your vulnerability or helplessness is essential for renewal and healing.

## ACKNOWLEDGING YOUR INNOCENCE AND SEEKING HEALING

Embracing the truth of your innocence is a critical step on the journey to healing. Like the woman in the field, you found yourself in a situation beyond your control. You suffered through it until you could escape, possibly having to regain coherence or consciousness first. Accepting that you didn't cause your assault will help to lift the burden of false guilt and allow you to embrace God's comfort and healing.

Understanding your experience through the lens of Deuteronomy 22:25–27 can be transformational.

However, it's also helpful to seek support from others who have walked through abuse or assault and found renewal in Christ. As you process your trauma, exercise wisdom in choosing whom to trust with your story.

Be discerning about sharing with individuals who may have ties to both you and the abuser, as they could feel pressured to "stay neutral." Ultimately, God desires to be your refuge—a safe place where you can express your thoughts and feelings without fear of judgment. Those you confide in should reflect these Christ-like qualities, providing a space of compassion and understanding.

If you haven't spoken much (or at all) about the abuse, seek out a trusted Christian friend or mentor who can offer comfort and guidance. Spending time reflecting on Scripture, praying, or even reading this book with someone who shares a similar journey can provide deep healing. This shared experience can also help reaffirm your innocence and provide you with much encouragement. Remember, you are not alone. With God and the help of others you trust, there is always a path forward toward healing and restoration.

## FOR REFLECTION

1. What has caused you to question whether your experience was sexual abuse or assault?
2. How does understanding your innocence through the lens of Deuteronomy 22:25–27 bring you hope or comfort, and how will you embrace this truth?

Read the following passages about God being a place of safety, refuge, and trust. Write out one or two truths you learn from them and how you will apply those truths to your life.

- Psalm 71:1–4
- Psalm 91:1–2

## FURTHER READING*

- Pamela Gannon and Beverly Moore, *In the Aftermath: Past the Pain of Childhood Sexual Abuse* (Focus Publishing), 2017.
- David Powlison, *Sexual Assault: Healing Steps for Victims* (New Growth Press), 2010.

* While the author believes the resources suggested here (and at the end of each chapter) uphold biblical truth and adhere to the integrity of God's Word, their inclusion is not meant to endorse any particular author or ministry.

## Chapter 2

# WAS IT MY FAULT?

Years later, after contemplating what happened to me in high school that night behind the movie theater, this question entered my mind: Was it my fault? Was it what I wore that night? Had I somehow given him the impression that I wanted to do those things? I never said I did, and he never asked for my consent.

My self-questioning turned into self-blame. I thought, *Well, Camille, if you had been where you were supposed to be in the first place, that wouldn't have happened.* Blaming yourself when you have been violated is a common occurrence for victims.

The story of Dinah in Genesis 34 is a sobering account of sexual violence. Dinah's experience resonates with many who struggle with feelings of false guilt and self-blame. A careful study of the Scriptures will help you understand how easily someone suffering from sexual trauma can become lost within their own story. Dinah's story unfolds this way:

> Dinah, Leah's daughter whom she bore to Jacob, went out to see some of the young women

> of the area. When Shechem son of Hamor the Hivite, a prince of the region, saw her, he took her and raped her. He became infatuated with Dinah, daughter of Jacob. He loved the young girl and spoke tenderly to her. "Get me this girl as a wife," he told his father Hamor.
>
> Jacob heard that Shechem had defiled his daughter Dinah, but since his sons were with his livestock in the field, he remained silent until they returned. Meanwhile, Shechem's father Hamor came to speak with Jacob. Jacob's sons returned from the field when they heard about the incident and were deeply grieved and angry. For Shechem had committed an outrage against Israel by raping Jacob's daughter, and such a thing should not be done. (Genesis 34:1–7)

## WAS IT YOUR FAULT? LEARNING FROM DINAH'S STORY

The historical account of Dinah's rape is God's gracious way of affirming to us that fault lies solely with the perpetrator of abuse or assault. But read just a handful of Bible commentaries on Genesis 34 and you will see the misinterpretation of the text and an obvious lean toward victim blaming. Dinah's part in her own story is skewed into some form of sin that wrongly places the blame on her.

One commentator veers far off course, reading too much into the original text when he says, "Indulged children, like Dinah, often become a grief and shame to their families. Her pretense was, to see the daughters of the land, to see how they dressed, and how they danced, and what was fashionable among them; she went to see, yet that was not all, *she went to be seen too. She went to get acquaintance with the Canaanites, and to learn their ways.* See what came of Dinah's gadding" (emphasis mine).[1] But this is not what the Bible actually says, and it's not what we are to believe about Dinah's tragic story.

Bible scholars put Dinah's age somewhere between thirteen and sixteen years old. She might have been full of curiosity (the text doesn't actually say that), but she was definitely full of sexual innocence. She was a virgin. Her purity is likely what made her the prey of a powerful, predatory prince. The Bible says that Shechem "saw her, he took her and raped her." Shechem felt entitled. So much so that he believed he could take Dinah and violate her without fear of consequence. Then he demanded that his father arrange a marriage so that he could keep having his way with her. His words to his father reveal his self-centeredness and arrogance: "Get me this girl as a wife."

When Dinah's father and brothers found out what happened to her, they didn't shame her or blame her. The Bible says her brothers were "deeply grieved and angry." Moses, the writer of Genesis under the inspiration of the Holy Spirit, wrote in Genesis 34:7, "For Shechem had committed *an outrage* against Israel by *raping* Jacob's daughter, and *such a thing should not be done*" (emphasis mine). Scripture doesn't blame Dinah at all. No one else in the text blamed her either—and neither should we.

## THE PROBLEM WITH VICTIM BLAMING

When you survey the cultural climate regarding victim blaming versus victim advocacy, the latter is often the least chosen response after sexual abuse or assault has occurred. For instance, in cases where individuals are assaulted after consuming alcohol or attending a party, there is a tendency to question the victim's judgment, rather than focus on the assailant's actions. This mirrors the misguided interpretation that Dinah was somehow to blame for her assault because she chose to visit the Canaanite women.

Just read a string of social media comments about allegations of sexual assault perpetrated by someone famous. You'll soon see how our current culture tends to question what the victim was doing or wearing, or whether there was an established romantic relationship between the assailant and the victim. Modern society could take a cue from Israel when it comes to assisting victims by rightly being outraged and declaring, "Such a thing should not be done!" Then perhaps we would have better advocacy in seeking justice for victims who often must face their abusers in court and testify against them. We will explore the topic of justice further in chapter 7.

## WHAT ABOUT WHAT HAPPENED TO YOU?

The Bible records other disturbing stories of rape: the gang rape of a woman in Judges 19 and the rape of King David's daughter Tamar by her half-brother Amnon in 2 Samuel 13. In these biblical accounts of rape, strong language is used to condemn the assaults. If you have been sexually traumatized, God wants you to know he declares that what has happened to you is *evil*, *outrageous*, and *something that should never happen*.

As you think through the circumstances leading up to Dinah's assault and then consider your own sexual trauma, I hope God will use insights from her story to help clarify any confusion you may have regarding who is to blame. I know that I was greatly confused over who was to blame for my assault.

For the record, let me be clear that I was foolish and wrong for not obeying my parents. I was curious about the handsome stranger from school. It is not wrong to have feelings of attraction or to be curious. These are natural inclinations, and they move us toward the person to whom we are attracted. This is by God's design, but we must remember that we live in a fallen world with faulty feelings and flawed people. I did not use wisdom with my feelings of attraction and curiosity. I also sinned by disobeying my parents and not being where I was supposed to be that night—inside the movie theater. My sinful decision put me in a precarious situation. Maybe you also put yourself in a precarious position when your abuse occurred.

While it may sound completely irrational to someone who has not been subjected to continuous abuse, some women have told me that they began making themselves available to their abuser after the initial act of abuse occurred. Repeated molestation can have a conditioning effect on a child—even one as young as an infant—resulting in the child seeking out sexual stimulation. A child exhibiting this behavior doesn't truly understand what they are doing and should not be blamed. They need loving and patient correction and teaching about God's purposes for our bodies. It may take time and additional patience to overcome this conditioning.[2]

## GOD'S GOOD GIFT OF SEX GONE BAD

Being innocent and curious or being conditioned to sexual stimulation as a child doesn't mean the abuse was your fault. It means that an abuser has used something meant to be good for their own evil purposes. Our good God created sex between a husband and a wife to be pleasurable. To put it bluntly, by design sex feels good. If human beings didn't enjoy sexual activity, it would be difficult to fulfill God's command to "be fruitful and multiply" (Genesis 1:28; 9:1). If sex were not pleasurable, a married couple would have trouble desiring to be sexually intimate often enough to procreate and advance human flourishing. Beyond procreation, sex is also meant to strengthen and nourish the bond between a husband and wife as they enjoy intimacy together.

Sadly, because of the fall of humanity, men and women have misused sex for selfish gain, as in cases of sexual abuse and assault. And yet the body still knows that sexual activity can feel good. A victim may feel ashamed about initiating sexual activity with their abuser, not recognizing that their body has become conditioned to sexual stimulation. Then, in a court case, a young witness may be peppered with questions of this nature by a defense attorney: "But didn't you begin to go into his bedroom?" or "Didn't you wait for him on the couch in the middle of the night?"

If this describes your experience, you may have questioned your innocence, believing the abuse was your fault. However, a victim is never at fault for the abuse suffered. Initially, I called into question my innocence. However, my foolishness and disobedience didn't *cause* the assault; my assailant caused it. Dinah didn't do anything to cause her sexual trauma, and neither did you.

Implying that Dinah's presence with the Canaanite women somehow contributed to her assault is deeply flawed reasoning. This kind of faulty thinking perpetuates the pervasive myth in our society that a victim's actions can invite sexual violence. They do not.

## THE PERPETRATOR'S GUILT

The Bible makes it unequivocally clear that Shechem's actions were wrong. God chose to use these words to record the incident in Genesis 34:2: "Shechem . . . saw her, he took her and raped her." The focus of this passage is on his aggressive and violent behavior toward Dinah. Shechem's subsequent affection and desire to marry Dinah do not excuse his crime; rather, this highlights his audacity to rationalize his actions and then seek to make amends afterward by speaking "tenderly to her" (v. 3).

Perpetrators often do this by saying things like "I'm so sorry," "I don't know what came over me," or "It'll never happen again." These statements sound similar to Shechem's interaction with Dinah after he violated her—trying to make up for his evil actions while attempting to get her to stay with him. Yet her brothers' reaction of shock and anger upon learning of Dinah's assault underscores the severity of Shechem's crime. It speaks volumes as to her innocence and the perpetrator's blame, reinforcing the truth that the fault lies entirely with Shechem.

## IF YOU STILL FEEL GUILTY ABOUT WHAT HAPPENED

While the Bible underscores that a victim is not to blame regarding their abuse, you may still feel guilty for what happened. Perhaps you feel convicted over something you said or did to draw attention to yourself, accidentally putting yourself in harm's way, or not using wisdom or discernment in a certain situation.

If you feel convicted over any choices you made before the abuse, know that God's grace covers every sin. You can bring any burdens of guilt or shame to him, and he will forgive and cleanse you completely (1 John 1:9). Most importantly, no choice you made justifies what was done to you—the sin is solely on the abuser. After I confessed disobeying my parents and acting foolishly, I was able to receive God's forgiveness and move past the false guilt I was carrying over the abuse somehow being my fault. I dealt with my guilt about making a bad choice to be somewhere I shouldn't have been. But I made sure not to continue feeling guilty for what had been done to me. Had I held onto false guilt over sin that wasn't mine, I would have been unable to see my need for God's healing of the sin done against me. Once I did that, I found the renewal I had been searching for.

## THE REALITY OF COERCION AND POWER

At the heart of sexual violence is power and control. Sexual predators exploit their victims, who may be physically weaker, socially marginalized, or otherwise vulnerable. This dynamic is evident in Dinah's story, where Shechem, a prince, capitalizes on his privilege and status to overpower her. Similarly, many modern-day assaults involve perpetrators who exploit their authority—a supervisor at work, a coach, a teacher, a doctor, a pastor, or another church leader.

Consider the numerous high-profile cases of sexual assault in the workplace, where powerful figures have preyed upon their subordinates. In these scenarios, victims often face immense pressure not to report, fearing retaliation. If a pastor or ministry leader abuses a congregant, the victim can be intimidated, afraid of being blamed for causing a church or ministry-wide scandal. Because of their status, the assailant may also threaten to ruin the victim's reputation within their local community, shaming them into silence.

Perhaps someone with familial status is the abuser—a father, husband, uncle, or older/stronger brother. Being abused by a family member can be especially devastating due to the abuser's proximity to the victim—living together in a home or having to attend frequent family functions together. In these cases, it is common for an abuser to manipulate a victim's thoughts and emotions to keep the abuse hidden from the rest of the family.

## THE IMPORTANCE OF AFFIRMING YOUR INNOCENCE AND SEEKING RENEWAL

To counteract victim blaming, it is essential to self-affirm your innocence. When correctly interpreted, Dinah's story is a powerful tool to help with this. Even if you made decisions that placed you in harm's way, the perpetrator is solely responsible for the abuse or assault. Understanding that the abuse wasn't your fault is central to finding renewal and embracing God's comfort and hope after sexual trauma.

The story of Dinah in Genesis 34 provides a profound biblical lens through which to view the issue of sexual violence and victim blaming. By examining Dinah's story, you can draw parallels to your own. Reaffirming the truths you learn from the Bible—that the source of sexual trauma lies entirely with the perpetrator—will help you move forward. Regardless of your actions or decisions leading up to the abuse or assault, God wants you to understand that you are not to blame for what happened to you—and you never were.

## FOR REFLECTION

Use the following exercise to help you sort out the details of what happened to you.

1. First, make a general list of things the assailant did to sin against you (e.g., manipulation, physical overpowering, the abuse/assault itself, and any coverup or coercion afterward).
2. Go through the list and agree with God that these actions were the perpetrator's fault. Ask God to heal you from the pain that each of these caused you.
3. Next, make a list of anything you did before, during, and after the abuse/assault that you feel shame or guilt over.
4. Then write beside each one "I didn't know that was wrong" or "I did know that was wrong."

5. Go through the list and agree with God that you are innocent about the things you didn't know were wrong. Then agree with God about the things you did know were wrong. Tell him that because Jesus died on the cross to pay for your sins, you choose to receive his forgiveness for each of these sins. And then walk in the freedom that Jesus has provided (Galatians 5:1).

Read the following passages about guilt and innocence. Write out one or two truths that you learn from them. Then ask God for his help to live them out.

- Proverbs 17:15
- 1 John 1:9

## FURTHER READING

- Justin S. Holcomb and Lindsey A. Holcomb, *Rid of My Disgrace: Hope and Healing for Victims of Sexual Assault* (Crossway, 2011).
- David Powlison, *Innocence Lost: Rebuilding after Victimization* (New Growth Press, 2011).

# Chapter 3

# WHY DID THIS HAPPEN TO ME?

My assault is not the only intense suffering I've endured. In my late teens, I experienced two crisis pregnancies. During my high school graduation, I walked across the stage to receive my diploma six months pregnant with my daughter Lauren. Her father was no longer in the picture. After she was born, I raised her as a single mom with the help and support of my parents.

When Lauren was about eight months old, I began dating again. I longed for a future where I could be a wife, and now I had a daughter who needed a father. Eventually, I met a young man whose family seemed to share similar values to mine, though he wasn't a believer. Our relationship quickly became sexual, and within just one month, I found myself pregnant again.

At first, we were excited. We talked about our future, planned to get married, and even became engaged. But when my parents found out about the pregnancy, they pressured me to have an abortion. They wanted me to focus on raising Lauren and finishing my college education. With life's mounting pressures, my relationship with my boyfriend started to unravel. We argued constantly. At one point, I thought about ending the relationship, but I was afraid of being alone, so I kept pushing forward, trying to make it work.

Little did I know that a dark side lurking within him would alter the course of all our lives forever. One night he was taking care of Lauren while I was at work. In the middle of my shift, my mom came to my workplace. I could tell that she was trying to stay calm, but I knew something was wrong. She said the words no mother ever wants to hear: "You have to come to the hospital. Something has happened to Lauren."

Within twenty-four hours, the devastating truth came to light—my boyfriend had sexually assaulted and shaken Lauren to death. I was completely shattered. It felt like my entire world had come crashing down around me, like my life was truly ending. I had to face the unimaginable and say goodbye to my little girl as the doctors let me hold her little body, her head covered with bruising.

As the police searched for and eventually arrested my now ex-boyfriend, I was left to make Lauren's funeral arrangements. In the midst of this unimaginable grief, my parents continued to suggest that I should have an abortion. Four days after burying my daughter, overwhelmed by pain and confusion, I made the decision to go through with it.

I had lost so much in such a short time. In the weeks and months that followed, I was swallowed up in grief.

My heart cried out to God over and over, *Why? Why did this happen to me?* If you have suffered sexual trauma, you may know this feeling all too well.

The question, Why did this happen to me? is the heart cry of many who have endured unimaginable trauma, especially the pain of sexual abuse or assault. It's a question that rises from the depths of human suffering. To begin to understand the answer, we must look to the beginning of human history, found in Genesis 1–3—the story of the fall. This account of the first man and woman provides profound insight into the origins of suffering, sin, and the hope of redemption.

## A PERFECT BEGINNING

The Bible opens with the scene of a pristine paradise. In Genesis 1, we read that God created the heavens and the earth, filling them with life and beauty. Human beings, made in God's image, were created with dignity, purpose, and the privilege of living in intimate fellowship with their loving Creator.

Adam and Eve, the first humans, lived in the garden of Eden—a place of peace, abundance, and unhindered communion with God. In this perfect state, there was no suffering, no pain, and no violation of one another. The relationships between husband and wife and between humanity and God were characterized by trust, respect, and love. Sexual intimacy in marriage was a gift from God to the couple, designed to be pure and good, meant for the mutual joy and pleasure of husband and wife (1 Corinthians 7:3).

## SIN SHATTERED ALL THINGS, INCLUDING SEX

This idyllic existence between God and humankind, as well as between husband and wife, was shattered by sin (Genesis 3:7–8). In Eden, Satan—who had taken the form of a serpent—tempted Adam and Eve to eat from the forbidden tree of the knowledge of good and evil. Succumbing to temptation, they committed an act of disobedience that introduced sin into the world.

With sin came a cascade of consequences: shame, guilt, and the fracturing of relationships, including sexual intimacy. I find it interesting that the very first consequence Adam and Eve experienced was the tainting of their once-pure relationship. Both realized their nakedness and sought to cover themselves, symbolizing the loss of innocence and the introduction of shame into the human experience. Their relationship with God was marred by their sin; fear and hiding replaced their once-perfect fellowship with him. In that one act of disobedience, everything became broken.

## THE SHOCK WAVES OF SIN

The fall was not an isolated event; it sent shock waves throughout creation (Romans 5:12; 8:20–22). Sin now affects every facet of human life and relationships. The complete peace and tranquility that the first humans enjoyed with God in Eden now seems like a distant memory—a fairy tale even—when you look around at a world filled with brokenness, pain, and suffering. This brokenness manifests in many tragic forms, including the horrific reality of sexual abuse and assault.

In a post-fall world, people are capable of inflicting tremendous harm upon one another. The dignity and sanctity of those created in God's image are profaned. Sexual abuse grieves God deeply because it violates the sacredness of another person's body and soul, leaving devastating emotional, mental, and sometimes physical scars.

## TRYING TO UNDERSTAND WHY

When grappling with the question, Why did this happen to me? it is essential to understand that the abuse or assault endured does not reflect a person's worth or value in God's eyes. Rather, it is a tragic consequence of living in a fallen world, where sin and evil now exist. While the fall explains the presence of sin and suffering, it does not diminish the dignity and worth of those who have experienced sexual trauma.

Sexual abuse represents a heinous distortion of the goodness and beauty of sex as intended by God. It perverts his divine gift meant for the sacred covenant of marriage between a husband and wife. Sexual intimacy was designed to express the deepest connection between two people—the knowing of each other—a profound oneness that reflects the spiritual oneness Christians experience with their Creator and Savior, Jesus Christ (1 Corinthians 6:17). This is why Jesus is referred to in the Bible as the Bridegroom and the church as his bride (Isaiah 61:10; Mark 2:18–20; John 3:29; Ephesians 5:22–23; Revelation 19:6–9, 21:2).

Realizing that God's design for sexual intimacy in marriage mirrors the spiritual intimacy Christ has with his followers sheds light on why the enemy attacked Adam and Eve in Eden. Satan seeks to destroy all of God's good creation, particularly human beings because they are created in his image. Our mortal enemy seeks to do this in one of the most traumatic ways possible—through sexual sin. The pain and trauma suffered by victims of abuse and assault is a direct result of Satan's plot to destroy us.

## GOD'S HEART FOR THE BROKENHEARTED AND THE PROMISE OF REDEMPTION

Amid the darkness of sin and suffering, the Bible also reveals the light of hope. God's heart is for the hurting. Although Adam and Eve turned away from God in disobedience and every human being since then has done the same, God had a plan to rescue those broken by sin. Throughout Scripture, God shows himself to be a compassionate and loving Creator who deeply cares for the wounded. As we read in Psalm 34:18, "The Lord is close to the brokenhearted; he rescues those whose spirits are crushed" (NLT).

God's response to sin and suffering is not one of indifference; rather, he is actively involved in our redemption and healing. The narrative of the fall does not end in despair. In Genesis 3:15, we find the first glimmer of the hope of redemption, where God declares that the offspring of the woman will crush the serpent's head. This is a foreshadowing of Jesus Christ's coming. He did come, entering human history to ultimately defeat sin and death through his sinless life, sacrificial death on the cross, and glorious resurrection from the dead.

Jesus Christ, the Son of God, took on flesh and became like us to save us (Hebrews 2:14–18). Born into this world, he embraced our frailties and weaknesses while remaining fully God. In this human state, he endured the depths of human suffering, including his excruciating crucifixion. His profound suffering and sacrifice provided the way for our redemption *and* healing. As Isaiah 53:5 reminds us, "But He was pierced because of our transgressions, crushed because of our iniquities; punishment for our peace was on Him, and we are healed by His wounds."

Jesus's earthly ministry is marked by compassion, offering the promise of peace and healing to all who put their faith in him. For victims of sexual abuse, this promise shines as a beacon of hope. While the pain and trauma you have endured is real and profound, it does not have the final word in your life. Jesus's sacrifice on the cross proves that God is intimately acquainted with human suffering. Furthermore, Christ's resurrection from the dead demonstrates that he has the power to bring new life and wholeness. As 2 Corinthians 5:17 assures us, "Therefore, if anyone is in Christ, he is a new creation; old things have passed away, and look, new things have come."

## THE JOURNEY OF RENEWAL

Finding renewal after sexual trauma is a journey that often involves pain, struggle, and the need for support. It is essential to seek help from a trusted pastor, experienced biblical counselor, or trusted Christian friend who can provide guidance along the way. Healing requires processing the pain of the past, laying hold of a sense of worth and identity rooted in Jesus, and choosing forgiveness. If the phrase "choosing forgiveness" throws you into a panic, please pause and take a breath. We will explore these concepts more deeply in the chapters ahead, discussing how they may look for you.

The question, Why did this happen to me? is complex and deeply personal. The story of the fall in Genesis chapters 1–3 provides a framework for understanding the presence of sin and suffering in the world. Sexual abuse is a tragic consequence of the brokenness introduced by sin, but it does not define your worth or dictate your destiny.

Amid your pain, the Bible offers a profound message of hope in Christ's power to redeem and renew. God's heart is for those broken by sin—both their own sin *and* the sins committed against them. His promise of healing and restoration is available to all who seek him. While the journey to renewal after sexual trauma can be challenging, it is possible with the support of caring Christians and God's good care through a relationship with him fostered by prayer and reading his Word. The fallenness of humanity is not the end of the story; with Jesus, there is the promise of renewal—a new life with new beginnings.

## FOR REFLECTION

1. Read Psalm 34:1–10. Many of the Psalms were written by David as expressions of his emotions to the Lord in relation to his life experiences. Throughout his life, David faced relentless

pursuit by enemies—often those who had once been close to him. He was open and honest about expressing grief and frustration over his suffering and the betrayal he endured, yet he consistently returned to praising God for his wonderful attributes and care. As you read this psalm, take a moment to circle the truths about God that David emphasizes. Consider how these attributes provide comfort and strength in times of struggle.

2. After reading the passage in Psalm 34, try writing your own personal psalm to the Lord. It doesn't have to be lengthy; feel free to write just a few sentences or several—it's up to you. Pour out your heart to God, expressing your questions about the suffering and trauma you have endured. Remember to ask for his help and guidance as you navigate this journey of renewal.

## FURTHER READING

- Christopher Ash, *Trusting God in the Darkness: A Guide to Understanding the Book of Job* (Crossway, 2021).
- Robert K. Cheong, *Restoration Story: Why Jesus Matters in a Broken World* (New Growth Press, 2021).

# Chapter 4

## AM I DAMAGED BEYOND REPAIR?

In the previous chapters, I opened up about my struggle with sexual promiscuity as a teenager and how God, in his grace, introduced me to a godly man in my early twenties. I thank God that my husband didn't bring any sexual baggage with him, instead remaining a virgin until our wedding day. Though we experienced a bit of awkwardness with physical intimacy on our honeymoon, it was filled with tenderness and joy as we joined together as one. It was sweet and beautiful.

However, upon returning home from our honeymoon, it didn't take long for memories of my past sexual encounters to flood my mind during moments of intimacy with my husband. There were times my body would physically react—tensing up in ways that made me not want to be touched. This left me feeling guilty and confused, and it left him feeling rejected. I began to struggle to understand why something that should have been a beautiful expression of love now felt so wrong. Everything seemed off, plunging me into a dark emotional state.

Until that point, I hadn't fully recognized the extent to which the sexual assault I endured in high school had marred my understanding of God's design for sexual intimacy. Gradually, I came to see that my sexual trauma had not only shaped my past promiscuity but also cast a shadow over sex with my husband. I was left grappling with the painful consequences of sexual sin—both my own and that inflicted upon me. A deep fear took hold of my heart and mind: Would I ever experience the beautiful design for sexual intimacy that God intended for married couples?

Regardless of whether your trauma resulted from being groped, being raped, or another form of sexual abuse, the aftermath can leave profound wounds—physical, emotional, mental, and spiritual. The effects can manifest in myriad ways: an inability to trust, lingering physical injuries, nightmares, flashbacks, and panic attacks. Often these struggles are accompanied by the persistent question, Am I damaged beyond repair?

This chapter seeks to address this deeply personal and painful question through the lens of Scripture, focusing on the story of Tamar in 2 Samuel 13. By examining Tamar's experience, we can gain a clearer understanding of the impact of sexual trauma and discover biblical guidance for healing and renewal.

## THE TRAGIC STORY OF TAMAR

One of the most heart-wrenching stories in the Bible is the rape of Tamar, the daughter of King David and full sister of Absalom. Her half-brother, Amnon, harbored a sexual obsession for her. Many people mistakenly believe that sexual assault is most often perpetrated by strangers. However, statistics reveal that in eight out of ten cases, the assailant is someone known to the victim—just as Amnon was known to Tamar.[1]

In 2 Samuel 13:2, we read, "Amnon was frustrated to the point of making himself sick over his sister Tamar because she was a virgin, but it seemed impossible to do anything to her." This verse captures the extent of Amnon's fixation, showcasing how his obsession turned into a dark and destructive desire.

Much like the story of Dinah's assault in Genesis 34, Tamar's narrative involves a predatory prince. Amnon's infatuation with and lust for his half-sister distorted his thinking to such an extent that he was continually devising schemes to have sex with her. Yet every scenario he imagined to "do anything" to her felt unlikely, given that she was the virgin daughter of the king. Amnon thought it seemed impossible to get her alone because she was well guarded and under the protection of their father.

Amnon's lust begins to take a physical toll on him, so much so that his cousin Jonadab notices and asks Amnon why he appears ill. When Amnon discloses his failure to fulfill his sexual appetite with Tamar, his much craftier cousin devises an evil plot to overpower the unsuspecting Tamar while avoiding suspicion. In verse 5, we read Jonadab's deceptive advice: "Lie down on your bed and pretend you're sick. When your father comes to see you, say to him, 'Please let my sister Tamar come and give me something to eat. Let her prepare food in my presence so I can watch and eat from her hand.'"

Feigning illness, Amnon follows his cousin's suggestion and asks his father to send Tamar to his room to prepare food for him. Unbeknownst to the king—and everyone else—this ruse is a trap set for innocent Tamar (2 Samuel 13:6–9). King David unwittingly sends his beloved daughter straight into a vile scheme, unaware of the dark intentions lurking behind Amnon's request.

After Amnon commands everyone else to leave his chamber, Tamar is left completely vulnerable and helpless, and the trap snaps shut. In 2 Samuel 13:10–14, we read,

> Then he said to Tamar, "Now bring the food into my bedroom and feed it to me here." So Tamar took his favorite dish to him. But as she was feeding him, he grabbed her and demanded, "Come to bed with me, my darling sister." "No, my brother!" she cried. "Don't be foolish! Don't do this to me! Such wicked things aren't done in Israel. Where could I go in my shame? And you would be called one of the greatest fools in Israel. Please, just speak to the king about it, and he will let you marry me." But Amnon wouldn't listen to her, and since he was stronger than she was, he raped her. (NLT)

In analyzing this passage, we see how Amnon seizes the opportunity to exploit Tamar's vulnerable state, physically and verbally pressuring her with his forceful imposition to have sex with him: "he grabbed her and demanded." With much courage, Tamar resists him, rebuffing his intentions and then trying to appeal to his conscience. Her first response is a heartfelt "No, my brother!"—a cry that underscores her expectation that he, as her brother, should protect her rather than assault her.

Tamar then firmly rebukes him, stating, "Don't be foolish! Don't do this to me! Such wicked things aren't done in Israel." She further pleads with him, highlighting how his sinful actions will affect her. "Where could I go in my shame?" she asks, emphasizing the shame that would follow her. Furthermore, she warns him, "And you would be called one of the greatest fools in Israel," stressing the gravity of his sin and how it would affect his reputation, especially as a son of the king.

Finally, Tamar appeals to Amnon to do what is right, urging him to seek permission from their father, King David, to allow them to marry: "Please, just speak to the king about it, and he will let you marry me." While this plea may seem quite odd in our modern context, it holds incredible significance for the culture of ancient times. In that day and time, a woman who lost her virginity outside of marriage—whether willingly or forcefully—was often viewed as "damaged goods." It would become unlikely that any man would be willing to marry her, leaving her either completely destitute or at the mercy of a relative to take her into their home and care for her financially for the rest of her life. Tamar's desperate request reflects not only her innocence but also the hard reality that women faced in an era where immense value was placed on a woman's virginity.

Tragically, Tamar's resistance to her brother's unwanted advances and her desperate pleas for him to do the right thing go unheard. Following the assault, Amnon's twisted feelings of "love" toward Tamar quickly turn into intense hatred. He callously discards her, compounding her trauma with the pain of rejection and public shame. Tamar's response to this horrific act is a profound expression of grief and despair. In her anguish, she tears her ornate robe—a powerful symbol of her virginity and royal status—and covers her head with ashes, mourning the loss of her dignity, honor, and innocence (2 Samuel 13:18–19). This action reflects not only the intensity of her sorrow, but also the utter devastation of being violated, used, and then tossed aside.

## THE PHYSICAL, MENTAL, AND EMOTIONAL EFFECTS OF SEXUAL TRAUMA

Tamar's story powerfully illustrates the destructive effects of abuse and assault. Sexual trauma leaves physical, mental, and emotional wounds. The Bible teaches that Christians' bodies are temples of the Holy Spirit (1 Corinthians 6:19–20), carefully and purposefully created by God for good things. When someone is sexually abused or assaulted, the body is violated, leading to a range of physical consequences that underscore the gravity of being sinned against in such a harmful way.

Sexual trauma can manifest physically in various ways—chronic pain, headaches, and gastrointestinal issues, to name a few. The stress and anguish resulting from abuse or assault can also take a toll on the body's systems. The heart may race, muscles tense, and sleep become elusive, leading to fatigue and a weakened immune system. For women, sexual abuse can also result in reproductive health issues, including pelvic pain, transmission of an infection through sexual contact, menstrual irregularities, and challenges with intimacy in marriage.[2] These physical consequences reveal the far-reaching impact of sin on God's design for human sexuality, which he intended to be experienced within the covenant love of marriage between a husband and wife.

Moreover, the effects of sexual abuse are not limited to the immediate aftermath; they can persist for years, even decades. Many survivors struggle with eating disorders, substance abuse, or self-harm as they cope with lingering pain. These behaviors are often attempts to numb the mental and emotional agony that continues throughout their lives.

Survivors of abuse or assault often face a range of complex mental and emotional challenges, with shame being one of the most overwhelming responses. Before Amnon assaults her, Tamar's plea demonstrates the depth of a survivor's pain when she asks, "Where could I go in my shame?" (2 Samuel 13:13). The Hebrew word for *shame* here means "reproach" that rests upon the condition of shame, or disgrace.[3] Tamar's question echoes the experience of many survivors as they wrestle with feelings of worthlessness and disgrace, though the guilt is not theirs to bear.

Blaming yourself for the assault places the guilt on the wrong person and becomes a barrier to healing. It is important to remember that the guilt rightfully belongs to the one who sinned, not to the one who was sinned against. As Ezekiel 18:20 reminds us, "The righteousness of the righteous person will be on him, and the wickedness of the wicked person will be on him." Acknowledging that what happened to you was not your fault is an essential part of experiencing renewal and healing after sexual trauma.

The mental and emotional effects of sexual trauma are vast, and they can certainly feel overwhelming. One of the first casualties is trust, especially when the perpetrator is someone the victim once trusted. Fear and anxiety can loom large in the heart and mind with flashbacks or nightmares that draw from painful memories of past incidents. This often leads to hypervigilance, panic attacks, and avoidance of certain places or people associated with the trauma. Many survivors also wrestle with deep sadness, hopelessness, and feelings of worthlessness, which can spiral into depression and, in some cases, suicidal thoughts. Any of these effects can tempt you into social isolation, compounding your pain.

Perhaps one of the most detrimental effects of sexual abuse is the identity crisis that survivors may face. Sexual trauma can make individuals feel completely dehumanized and leave them struggling to believe they possess inherent worth and value. The Bible poignantly illustrates this in Tamar's story. After she was raped, Tamar went to live with her brother Absalom. The scars left by the assault are evident as Scripture tells us, "So Tamar lived as a desolate woman in the house of her brother Absalom" (2 Samuel 13:20). Her desolation mirrors the inner devastation that many survivors feel as they carry within themselves a shattered sense of self.

## FROM IDENTITY CRISIS TO IDENTITY IN CHRIST

Rather than being defined by a desolate life, you are invited by Jesus to find your true identity in him. You may struggle to believe who he says you are—and who he has created you to be—until you understand who he is and how he identifies with you in your sexual trauma.

It may surprise you to know that Jesus didn't endure only physical, mental, and emotional suffering on the cross—he also experienced the trauma of being naked and exposed to countless onlookers during his crucifixion. While many depictions of Christ on the cross show him wearing a loincloth, the reality of Roman crucifixion was far more brutal. Jesus was likely stripped completely naked, subjected to public shame and mockery as his tortured bare body was on display for all to see.[4] Though he wasn't sexually assaulted, his nakedness was exposed to the gaze and ridicule of countless onlookers as the crowds poured into Jerusalem for Passover. With his hands nailed down, he was left utterly vulnerable, unable to cover his nakedness. Our Savior knows what it means to be victimized and shamed.

While Tamar's story tragically ends in silence and desolation, your story doesn't have to. Jesus Christ went to the cross not only to bear the weight of sin, but also to carry the shame and suffering that sin brings. On the third day, he rose from the dead, securing victory over sin and death for all who trust in him. Because of his triumph over evil, you can turn to Christ, who understands your trauma and offers you a new identity in him—one of beloved child of God. It's a wonderful invitation to the hope of renewal and healing that can only be found in Jesus.

## BIBLICAL STEPS TOWARD HEALING AND RENEWAL

The first step toward healing is to honestly acknowledge the pain and trauma you've endured. Tamar's grief and anguish were real and profound. As you seek renewal, it's essential to recognize that Scripture validates these emotions. Denying your suffering or downplaying your pain will only hinder your healing. Jesus invites you to bring your hurt to him, where you will find endless love and compassion.

Renewal begins by drawing near to God and seeking his nearness through his Word and in honest, heartfelt prayer. Psalm 34:18 promises us that the Lord is close to the brokenhearted, and 2 Corinthians 1:3–4 reminds us that he desires to comfort those who are suffering with all of the comfort he has to give. Turning to Jesus in your distress provides the strength and peace that your soul longs for. Jesus sees your pain, identifies with your suffering, and cares deeply about your healing.

It is important to understand that sexual abuse does not diminish your worth or alter this identity. The Bible affirms your worth. You are made in God's image (Genesis 1:27), and are incredibly valuable in his sight (1 Peter 2:9). You are still precious to God, beloved and cherished by him, and your value remains unchanged despite the trauma you have experienced.

Additionally, in Christ, there is the promise of a new identity with complete restoration. As 2 Corinthians 5:17 declares, "Anyone who belongs to Christ has become a new person. The old life is gone; a new life has begun!" (NLT). As a new person, those who have suffered the devastation of past sexual trauma can find hope in Christ's redemptive power and the transforming nature of his love.

The question, Am I damaged beyond repair? is one that resonates with many who have endured sexual abuse. Tamar's story shows us the heartbreaking reality of the physical, mental, and emotional effects of sexual trauma, but Scripture doesn't leave us there. The Bible extends tremendous hope to those who put their faith in Jesus. You are not defined by your trauma, but by your new identity in Christ. As God's child, you are cherished beyond measure.

God's answer to the question, Am I damaged beyond repair? is clear: You are not. Through Jesus, he offers you comfort, strength, and the promise of new life filled with eternal hope. Seek him, and you will find the healing and renewal that your heart longs for.

## FOR REFLECTION

1. How have you suffered physically, mentally, and emotionally from sexual trauma?
2. How do you relate to Tamar's story? What do you relate to in Christ's experience during his crucifixion?

Read the following Scriptures and reflect on how God works to bring about good in your life, even amid your suffering. Write out one or two truths that you learn from these Scriptures and how you will apply these truths to your daily life.

- Isaiah 61:1–3
- John 10:10

## FURTHER READING

- Diane Langberg, *Suffering and the Heart of God: How Trauma Destroys and Christ Restores* (New Growth Press, 2015).
- Timothy S. Lane, *PTSD: Healing for Bad Memories* (New Growth Press, 2012).

## Chapter 5

# WHAT IF I HAVE A NEGATIVE VIEW OF MY BODY?

By the time I reached fifth grade, I had heard various crude jokes and perverse talk circulating among my classmates about male and female body parts. Around this same time, I began asking my mom about the birds and the bees, driven by a genuine curiosity about the differences between male and female bodies and how babies were made. Though I didn't realize it at that age, I was searching for the truth about human sexuality. Everything I was hearing at school painted female and male anatomy and sex in a dirty light. Of course, there was no way I was going to disclose to my mom all the awful things that had been poured into my mind by my peers at school. I was too embarrassed.

My mom merely handed me an illustrated children's book about puberty and sex and left me to navigate its pages alone. After that, I don't recall any meaningful conversations, and my parents didn't seem very approachable or open to questions. It would be up to me—with the unhelpful assistance of my friends and peers—to piece together an understanding of sex and sexuality.

When I was twelve, I came to know Jesus as my Lord and Savior while attending a summer youth camp. Throughout my middle and high school years, our weekly church youth group meetings and occasional events seemed to have this teaching on repeat: Don't have sex until you're married. If you do, it's a sin. Yet, no one ever shared *why* sex was to be reserved for marriage, or *how* to wait until marriage to have sex or engage in sexual activity.

I knew one thing at that age: the curiosity I had in elementary school about sex had quickly morphed into a cloak of shame. Whenever we heard mention of sex, it was always in a sinful context. Up to that point, I had never heard that sex could be good and that God designed it to be its very best within a Christian marriage. Because I knew sex was wrong before marriage and I didn't want anything bad to happen to me—and I wanted to make God happy—I was committed to wait. But I had no road map for waiting.

For as long as I can remember, I wanted to get married someday. But what was the path of sexual purity supposed to look like? Oh, how I wish someone had taught me how to have a God-honoring dating relationship while navigating sexual pressure and temptation.

Before the sexual assault in high school, I had another bad experience when I was transitioning from elementary school to middle school and had begun to enter puberty. On this occasion, my parents were invited to play board games at the home of some church friends. Their daughter and I were good friends, so I was eager to go hang out with her. When we arrived, another couple was there with their teenage son. He was sixteen and quite handsome. I was smitten with him, and he knew it.

The three of us hung out in the back bedroom. He sat on the bed watching TV while my friend and I sat on the floor playing a game. After a while, he asked if I wanted to sit on the bed with him and look through a photo album. I jumped at the chance to sit next to him. As we flipped through the book, his hand gently slipped between my knees and he began lightly rubbing my leg. I was flushed with excitement. After all, I had seen lots of dating and married couples put their hands on each other's knees. The excitement quickly turned to panic as he kept moving his hand further and further up my inner thigh. I kept scooting back, away from his advancing hand, until my back was against the headboard and I had nowhere else to go.

He asked my friend to get him something from the kitchen. After she left, he asked me, "Do you want me to stop?" "Yes," I said. "Are you a prude?" he inquired. "I don't know what that means," I replied. He removed his hand as my friend walked back into the room. "She doesn't know what *prude* means," he told her. Then they both proceeded to explain its meaning. Thankfully, nothing happened after that, but I remember the embarrassment and unease I felt. His questioning of my reserved nature made me wonder whether something was wrong with me or my body.

## DISTORTED VIEWS

Experiencing sexual trauma from abuse or assault can deeply impact the way you think and feel about your body. Sexual perpetrators often manipulate their victims into believing that nonconsensual touches are expressions of "love" or "affection." (Of course, if you were a child when the abuse occurred, the law states that you cannot give consent to an adult by the nature of your age.) The sexual predator's manipulative narrative is an attempt to contradict one's instinct to protect the body and sexual innocence. An assailant can disarm their victim if they succeed in convincing them that certain touches are an appropriate display of affection. A victim might not realize that they were deceived until they reach adulthood. Only then does it become clear that their views about the body and sex have been distorted.

Furthermore, because God intends for our bodies to be kept holy to glorify him (1 Corinthians 6:18–20), by his design, we inherently try to protect and care for them (Ephesians 5:29). Naturally, we expect others to respect our bodies as well. When someone violates this sanctity through sexual abuse, we experience a profound loss of protection and care, leaving us with an unsettling sense that something is off.

Sexual trauma often distorts our perception of self. It's common for survivors to have feelings of shame, disgust, or disconnection from their bodies. When your body has been violated, your heart and mind can grapple with how to reconcile the experience with your physical form. Some may respond by seeking to reclaim control of their bodies, showing them off for the purpose of refusing unwanted sexual advances. This may seem counterintuitive after abuse. However, those who feel that their bodily autonomy was taken may imagine this will give them a sense of redemption and regained personal power.

Conversely, others may develop disdain for their bodies, opting to cover up in baggy clothes, or for some women, binding their chests to make them less visible. Victims—both female and male—might resort to punishing their bodies post-trauma. They may develop eating disorders such as anorexia or bulimia.

Overexercising can be another way to punish the body, causing unhealthy weight loss. In contrast, some may find themselves overeating with limited physical activity. Still others may turn to self-injury, inflicting pain on their bodies or destroying their appearance through cutting, burning their skin, plucking their hair or eyelashes, etc. Body modification through tattoos, piercings, or cosmetic surgery can also be a way to exert control or mask pain, though not everyone who modifies their body has experienced abuse.

## RENEWING YOUR MIND

God doesn't want you to misuse (show off) or abuse (punish) your body—especially when it has already endured so much harm because of someone else's sin. Instead, he calls you to view your body as sacred and good. In Romans 12:1, the apostle Paul states, "Therefore, brothers [and sisters], by the mercies of God, I urge you to present your bodies as a living sacrifice, holy and pleasing to God; this is your spiritual worship." This is how God wants you to view your body now.

But Satan seeks to undermine your ability to worship and honor God in every area of your life, including how you view and treat your body. The devil tries to exploit our suffering to plant lies in our minds about our identity and worth. These insidious lies can morph into negative thoughts about our bodies. Scripture reminds us that Satan is a deceiver (John 8:44), and we must combat his lies with the truth of God's Word and through prayer. As 2 Corinthians 10:3–5 says, "For though we live in the body, we do not wage war in an unspiritual way, since the weapons of our warfare are not worldly, but are powerful through God for the demolition of strongholds. We demolish arguments and every high-minded thing that is raised up against the knowledge of God, taking every thought captive to obey Christ."

But how do you do this? You renew your mind by taking a negative thought about your body, correcting it according to what the Bible says, and asking for help from God and others who love him to see yourself as God sees you. He has given you these wonderful means of grace to help you! Then you seek to align your life to God's truth by seeking to care for your body—thereby honoring him.

Holding extreme views about your body after enduring abuse—whether seeing it as an object to be displayed, a source of shame, or something to be punished—saddens God and dishonors his image in you. To be created in God's image means that your body has inherent value and dignity, regardless of what you have experienced. Embracing this foundational truth will allow you to renew your understanding of the body, shifting from self-loathing to healthy stewardship of it.

The Bible affirms that every human being has been fearfully and wonderfully made by God. In Psalm 139:13–14, the psalmist declares, "For it was You who created my inward parts; You knit me together in my mother's womb. I will praise You because I have been remarkably and wonderfully made. Your works are wonderful, and I know this very well." This verse serves as a powerful reminder that your body is not beyond repair. Rather, it is a good creation, intentionally crafted by God and entrusted to your care.

## A BIBLICAL VIEW OF YOUR BODY

God has entrusted us with our bodies, calling us to steward them well. After experiencing sexual trauma, it's essential to renew your mind with God's truth so you will have the desire to care for the body he has given you. The apostle Paul reminds us of the importance of this in 1 Corinthians 6:19–20, where he says, "Don't you realize that your body is the temple of the Holy Spirit, who lives in you and was given to you by God? You do not belong to yourself, for God bought you with a high price. So you must honor God with your body" (NLT).

You may have heard the phrase "Your body is your temple" in advertisements for hygiene products, but that's not true according to the Bible. God declares that a Christian's body is the temple of the Holy Spirit who dwells within them. The Greek word used for "temple" in this passage doesn't just refer to the structure originally located in Jerusalem; it refers to the most sacred place—the Holy of Holies—where God's presence was known to reside.[1]

Paul also teaches that since you were bought at a great cost—the precious blood of Jesus—you no longer belong to yourself. Your body is not a tool for self-glorification or self-harm, but a means to glorify and worship God. Consider trying to vandalize a church building. You would likely face consequences because the building isn't yours to alter. In the same way, your body was never created to be abused or violated by you or anyone else.

Your body was designed for God-honoring purposes, for good works that reflect his glory (Matthew 5:16, Ephesians 2:10, 1 Peter 2:12). You can use your body to serve others in need through simple yet meaningful acts—preparing a meal, helping with housework or yard work, writing a card of encouragement, creating a homemade gift, assisting someone with a move, or working on their car. Each of these acts is an opportunity to use your body as a tangible expression of God's love and grace to others.

As you begin to embrace this truth, your perspective on your body can shift. Instead of viewing your body as a source of pain, you can begin to view it as a valuable instrument for fulfilling God's good purposes. Your trauma does not define you—your identity is rooted in the God who lovingly created you to do good and calls you his own. He cares for you immensely and wants you to come to him with your deepest concerns and fears (1 Peter 5:7). Because of this, you can draw near to him right now.

## FOR REFLECTION

1. What negative thoughts about your body have taken root in your mind after experiencing sexual trauma?
2. What truths from God's Word will you replace those thoughts with?

Read the following Scriptures to learn how to renew your mind about how you view your body. Write one or two responses sharing how you can apply it to your life.

- Romans 6:13
- Ephesians 2:10
- Philippians 4:8

## FURTHER READING

- Amy Baker, *Relief without Cutting: Taking Your Negative Feelings to God* (New Growth Press, 2011).
- Lainey Greer, *Struggling with Body Image: Seeing What God Sees* (New Growth Press, 2024).
- Leslie Vernick, *Self-Esteem: Looking Up Instead of Looking Inside* (New Growth Press, 2016).

# Chapter 6

## HOW CAN I TRUST ANYONE AGAIN?

Experiencing sexual trauma profoundly impacts your ability to trust others, often creating social distances and divides that you may not know how to bridge. Maybe the abuse in your past has left you wondering if you even want to trust anyone again. For some, this distrust manifests as fear or even hostility toward the opposite sex. But when we address issues of trust through a biblical lens, we find a firm foundation in God's faithful love and the transformative power of the gospel of Jesus Christ.

In my years of counseling women who have suffered sexual abuse, I have observed a tendency to swing to extremes in their views about sex. Some become repulsed by the very thought of it, while others turn to sexual promiscuity, seeking validation and connection through physical intimacy. Few have discovered and sought to hold to God's view on sex—that it is holy and beautiful within marriage.

I know this struggle firsthand. My own view of intimacy and trust was tragically distorted, both by the assault and by my own sinful choices. I didn't trust men to want anything out of a relationship other than to use my body for their own selfish gain. So I began to use them for what I could get out of the relationship. This cycle of mutual misuse in sexual intimacy deepened my trust issues, leading me from one broken relationship to the next.

## WHAT IF MY DISTRUST CAUSES ME TO DISLIKE THE OPPOSITE SEX?

For some survivors of abuse, their response to trauma takes a different path than sexual promiscuity. Instead, they develop deep-seated distrust, which can evolve into dislike or even outright disdain for the opposite sex—often because their offender was of that gender. As fallen human beings living in a broken world, we build protective walls around our hearts, hoping to shield ourselves from further pain. For many female victims, the fear and distrust of men seems understandable considering that research shows men are the primary perpetrators of sexual abuse or assault. However, we must remember that women can also be offenders.[1] Those victimized by female offenders may carry their own struggles with distrust and hatred toward women.

Although my own assault didn't lead me to distrust men, the tragic assault and murder of my daughter did. After suffering her loss, I began to be suspicious of all men, viewing them as potential predators. Later, I learned that children of single mothers, particularly those with live-in partners, face an increased risk of being sexually abused.[2] This knowledge only fueled my distrust, reinforcing the walls I had built to protect myself and those I loved.

Because of this traumatic event in my life, I lived with the constant fear that a man could harm my children. Even now, after counseling countless women over the years, I still wrestle with a deep-seated distrust of men. Yet I know I must guard my heart against letting distrust harden into total disdain or hatred of the opposite sex.

Distrust can feel like a necessary shield, especially after trauma, as we try to protect ourselves from future harm. The Bible acknowledges the reality of evil and the suffering it causes. But there is a crucial difference between wisely guarding against potential danger and allowing our distrust to grow into a broad dislike or hatred of an entire gender. As followers of Christ, we are called to be wise yet loving (Matthew 5:43–45, James 3:13). God commands us to love our neighbors—including the opposite sex—because every person is made in his image (Mark 12:30–31).

## FEELING THE PAIN OF BETRAYAL

When someone we once trusted betrays us, the pain cuts deep. The stark statistics showing how often one gender perpetrates sexual assault can stir strong feelings of anger. Understandably, you may want to shout, "It shouldn't be this way!" You are right—it shouldn't. Life in this world is not as God originally intended it to be. Betrayal and abuse are the bitter fruits of sin, distorting the beauty of trust and the goodness of relationships.

In the beginning, God created a perfect man and a perfect woman to live in perfect harmony and unity (Genesis 1:26–31). Our good and loving Creator made them to work alongside one another as coequal colaborers striving to glorify their God in all that they did. God tasked Adam with the responsibility to work and care for the garden of Eden, protecting God's perfect paradise and everything in it. Eve was to be a helpful companion as together they took on the incredible feat of filling the earth and subduing it (Genesis 1:28; 2:15–24). Everything was good, right, and pure—until sin entered the picture in Genesis 3. It was then that betrayal, distrust, and brokenness first fractured the perfection God had designed.

The first consequence of Adam and Eve's rebellion against God was the corruption of their sexuality. Before sin entered the world, they were naked and felt no shame, enjoying pure intimacy as God intended (Genesis 2:25). But after they sinned, everything changed. Shame crept in, and they felt the need to cover themselves (Genesis 3:7). What had once been pure and innocent was now tainted. In an instant, their view of one another shifted—from seeing each other as God's beautiful gift to being tempted to view each other through the lens of perversion. Lustful or disgustful thoughts about sex would now engulf their hearts and minds—and this damaged view of sex would be passed on to the entire human race. Sin marred the marital intimacy that Adam and Eve had once enjoyed unhindered.

The tainting of sexual intimacy within marriage wasn't the only immediate casualty of Adam and Eve's sin. Instead of walking with God in peace, Adam and Eve hid from God's presence, now fearful of him (Genesis 3:8). In their guilt, they turned away from the intimate fellowship they once enjoyed with their Creator. Yet, even in their rebellion, God didn't abandon them. He called them out of hiding, inviting them to come to him (Genesis 3:9). Despite their betrayal, God reached out to them in love.

God held Adam and Eve accountable for their sin, rightly questioning their choice to rebel against his command not to eat from the tree of the knowledge of good and evil. Yet, in his justice, God also extended mercy by sparing them from immediate death—the very penalty they likely feared most (Genesis 2:16–17). Instead of turning in repentance to their Creator to receive forgiveness and grace, they turned on each other. Adam pointed the finger at Eve, insinuating that God himself was at fault for creating her as his wife (Genesis 3:9–12). In response, Eve shifted the blame to the crafty serpent (Satan) who had tricked her (Genesis 3:13; Revelation 12:9). This blame-shifting wasn't helpful to their cause. It never is.

Sin shattered the relationship between Adam and Eve and their bond with their loving Creator. Both the man and the woman were created by God to experience total joy and fulfilling intimacy in their relationship with him. Yet they had utterly betrayed him. Have you experienced the absolute devastation caused by the betrayal of someone you once trusted? God understands. He was betrayed in the garden of Eden, and he would endure betrayal again in another garden—the garden of Gethsemane.

The night before his crucifixion, Jesus met with his closest followers in a garden to pray, fully aware of the suffering that awaited him. In that moment, he sought comfort from his Father and support from his dearest friends—those who had even pledged to die with him (Matthew 26:35–46). If you are familiar with this account in Scripture, you know that Judas betrayed Jesus in that garden, leading an angry mob straight to him so they could arrest him (Matthew 26:47–50). However, Judas wasn't the only one to betray Christ; all of Jesus's closest followers also abandoned him that very night, just as Jesus had predicted (Matthew 26:31, 56). The Son of God was handed over to be executed—to die for our sins.

Jesus endured some of the most horrific treatment imaginable. He was mocked, spat upon, and punched in the face, and he had his beard ripped out. Flogged and stripped naked, he was taunted by the crowd of onlookers. Then he faced the excruciating agony of being crucified—all while bearing the weight of humanity's sin (Isaiah 53:3–12; Matthew 27:26–44; John 1:29). Jesus was abused and then murdered at the hands of those he had created to love and to be loved by (John 1:3; 1 John 4:19). God knows full well the pain of betrayal.

## WHO CAN YOU TRUST?

Since the fall, the thread of distrust has been woven into the fabric of human experience. The perfect trust between humanity and God and between man and woman has been ripped from us. Sin twists the human heart and mind, turning our sinful thoughts and desires into actions that cause others serious harm, including sexual abuse. We are all capable of inflicting the deepest and most deplorable wounds on each other. Yet when we are deeply wounded, it often reinforces our distrust of others. So what are we to do now? How can someone living with sexual trauma ever learn to trust again?

We can look to Jesus and his life here on earth as we learn to trust again after experiencing sexual trauma. Consider that all of Jesus's friends had run away at the time of his greatest need, abandoning him. When he hung on the cross, Jesus experienced complete abandonment. He cried out to his Father in mental, emotional, and spiritual anguish while enduring excruciating physical pain: "My God, my God, why have you abandoned me?" (Psalm 22:1 NLT).[3]

No human being has ever felt such darkness of the soul as Jesus did that day. Christ was utterly alone and forsaken by all, including his Father (Matthew 27:46). It's crucial to understand that God the Father did not betray Jesus on the cross. Instead, the Father turned away from his Son because, at that moment, Jesus became sin for us. God cannot dwell with or even look upon sin (Psalm 5:4; 34:16; Habakkuk 1:13; 2 Corinthians 5:21). The Father's turning away demonstrates that Jesus truly did take on the sin of the world, bearing the guilt and punishment for it (John 1:29).

Yet notice that soon after questioning his Father's abandonment, Jesus shouted from the cross, "Father, I *entrust* my spirit into your hands!" (Luke 23:46 NLT, emphasis mine). The Greek word used here for *entrust* means "to commit to one's charge."[4] Jesus fully understood that his Father was trustworthy and could be relied on to fulfill all his promises. In that moment, Jesus was holding on to the assurance that his Father had promised to raise him from the dead. Jesus's resurrection serves as a powerful affirmation that his sacrifice was sufficient to pay for the sins of humanity (Psalm 16:8–11; Hosea 6:1–2).

God has never betrayed anyone, and he never will, because he cannot sin (Hebrews 4:15; 1 Peter 2:22; 1 John 3:5). So when you grapple with the question about who you can trust, the answer is clear: You can trust God. I wrestled with this truth in the aftermath of my daughter's assault and murder. I understood that God is all-powerful and could have prevented what happened that day. Yet I came to recognize that it was a sinful human being who committed this act of evil against her, not God. A wicked man was to blame. So, while you may distrust a certain gender because of your sexual trauma, don't direct that distrust toward God. He has never sinned against you, and he never will. He alone is completely trustworthy.

## TRUSTING GOD

If suffering from sexual trauma has led you to distrust God, it will be helpful to spend time learning just how trustworthy he is. He wants you to get to know him more so that your faith and trust in him can grow. The truth is, the more you know someone, the more you begin to trust them. If you find areas in your life where you struggle to trust God, take the time to get to know him better. The Bible reassures you that if you seek him diligently, with your whole heart, he will be found by you (Proverbs 8:17; Isaiah 55:6; Jeremiah 29:13). Instead of distancing yourself from God, press in to discover more about him and his character.

The Bible reveals that we can trust God because of his unwavering faithfulness. Lamentations 3:22–23 beautifully reminds us, "The faithful love of the Lord never ends! His mercies never cease. Great is his faithfulness; his mercies begin afresh each morning" (NLT). Faithfulness is the exact opposite of betrayal.

God's love is another essential attribute highlighted in this passage. Scripture assures us that God's faithful love *never* ends and that his faithfulness is great! Because God's love never ceases, he is worthy of our trust. God can and should be trusted.

Not only is God faithful, but he is also true (Revelation 19:11). How do we know this? We have the eyewitness testimony of Jesus's love, faithfulness, and truthfulness recorded in the Gospels of Matthew, Mark, Luke, and John. If you are a Christian, you have experienced God's love and faithfulness firsthand when you placed your faith in Jesus to save you from sin and death. The ultimate testament to God's love for us is Jesus's sacrificial and substitutionary death on the cross for sinners like you and me. As John 3:16 emphatically states, "For this is how God loved the world: He gave his one and only Son, so that everyone who believes in him will not perish but have eternal life" (NLT). Now that's a love worth trusting!

## REBUILDING TRUST IN THE OPPOSITE SEX

Fallible human beings are not inherently trustworthy. God alone is completely trustworthy. Because he is trustworthy, we must believe that God originally created both males and females in his image—to be good. Although that image has been marred by sin, God still desires for us to value and respect all people—including people we distrust—because they bear his image.

This doesn't mean God commands that we trust untrustworthy people, or that we trust everyone unconditionally. We will encounter individuals who should not be trusted, whether it's because we don't know them well enough, they have yet to prove their trustworthiness, or their past actions reveal a pattern of untrustworthiness.

Esteeming God's design of males and females as his image bearers means that we cannot harbor dislike or hatred for an entire gender. The truth is that without Jesus, we would all remain dead in our sins and trapped forever in this fallen state. However, through Christ, both men and women can be redeemed from their sinful nature by placing their faith in him for salvation. Redeemed people can then be renewed in the way they view others—all for the glory of God. A vital part of this redemption and renewal involves learning to treat one another with Christlike love and respect.

Romans 12:2 wonderfully captures the transformation that occurs as you renew your mind. It says, "Let God transform you into a new person by changing the way you think. Then you will learn to know God's will for you, which is good and pleasing and perfect" (NLT). This transformation is a daily endeavor to align your thoughts and feelings with God's truth. As you immerse yourself in Bible reading and prayer, the Holy

Spirit works through these means of grace to reshape your understanding of yourself and others (Philippians 2:13). But this can't simply be a change in thought patterns. Being transformed to be more like Jesus in how you view and treat others requires spending focused time with him. It means pouring out your heart to him every day, telling him your struggles, asking for sustaining grace, and relying on his love (1 John 4:16). God doesn't only want your thoughts toward others to change—he wants your heart to reflect his.

As members of God's family, Christian men and women are called brothers and sisters in Christ (Romans 8:15; Galatians 3:28; 1 John 3:1–2). Knowing this, it's imperative that we hold to a Genesis 1 view of each other. We must remember that God created the two unique genders—male and female—to work *together* as his image bearers, filling the earth with his glory (Genesis 1:27–28; Isaiah 40:5; 43:7; Habakkuk 2:14). While you may find it difficult to trust every man or every woman due to the reality of sin and previously broken trust, you can trust your good God to redeem sinful people from both genders. His transformational work in their lives, as well as yours, is a powerful testimony to his grace and mercy.

So, what should you do when you are inclined to dislike a certain gender due to past sexual trauma? Fix your eyes on Jesus and trust his perfect plan of redemption, reconciliation, and renewal. Proverbs 3:5-6 encourages you: "Trust in the Lord with all your heart, and do not rely on your own understanding; *think about Him in all your ways*, and He will guide you on the right paths" (emphasis mine). As you place your trust in God, he will guide you in building relationships grounded in trust and love.

## FOR REFLECTION

1. What events in your life have tempted you to distrust God?
2. Which attribute of God do you need to learn about in order to know him better and trust him more?
3. How will you seek God's renewal to transform your perspective on people, particularly how you view your brothers and sisters in Christ?
4. Read Psalm 33:20–22, which speaks to the foundation of our hope and trust. Turn this into your own prayer, and ask God to move these truths from your head to your heart. Then ask him how to apply them to your life in actions.

## FURTHER READING

- Jerry Bridges, *31 Days Toward Trusting God* (NavPress, 2017).
- Elyse Fitzpatrick and Eric Schumacher, *Jesus and Gender: Living as Sisters and Brothers in Christ* (Kirkdale Press, 2022).
- Erin Wheeler, "It's Not Just You and Jesus," The Gospel Coalition (blog), July 8, 2022, thegospel coalition.org/article/not-you-and-jesus/.
- Jen Wilkin, *In His Image: 10 Ways God Calls Us to Reflect His Character* (Crossway, 2018).

# Chapter 7

## WILL JUSTICE BE DONE?

Cheyanne was molested as a child by a man who lived in the neighborhood. When she finally worked up the courage to tell her mom and dad, they didn't believe her. It wasn't until her older sister overheard the conversation and disclosed that she too had been molested by this man that Cheyanne's parents believed her and took action. She recalls her dad picking up the phone, calling the neighbor, and angrily telling him to stay away from his daughters. While the man didn't bother Cheyanne or her sister again, the police were never involved. Years later, Cheyanne heard about his continued abuse of other children in their community.

Ben's older brother would sexually gratify himself while touching Ben at the same time. Though scared of his brother, Ben bravely told their parents what had been happening. They scolded his brother, telling him to leave Ben alone. Then they warned Ben not to tell anyone else because it would cause trouble for the family. His parents never spoke about it after that. The abuse continued, and Ben's brother threatened him with violence if he spoke about it to their parents again.

Kelly's stepdad would slip into her bedroom at night, sit on the edge of her bed, and rub her belly. The seemingly innocent gesture soon turned into sexual molestation. Night after night, he would come into Kelly's room after her mom fell asleep. Soon Kelly began seeking out the touches from her stepdad because she had become sexually aroused by the abuse and wouldn't be able to sleep until afterward. When her mom found out about the abuse, she notified the authorities. For a time, Kelly's stepdad was removed from the home. As the family sought help from their church, Kelly's mom was urged to allow her husband—Kelly's abuser—back into the home to demonstrate forgiveness. Kelly felt betrayed and unprotected by the church. When she became an adult, Kelly left the church, angry at God and distrustful of church leadership.

Alice's youth pastor was close with her family. They often hung out at each other's homes to watch movies. On one occasion, while the families were together, Alice's mom got up and went into the kitchen to grab a snack. Meanwhile, Alice's youth pastor "accidentally" brushed his hand across her breast as he sat next to her. He quickly apologized for the incident. She believed him, until it happened again. That's when Alice decided to tell her mom and dad what he had done. The police were called, and the youth pastor was arrested. During the trial, the defense painted Alice as a flirtatious teen who was prone to exaggeration and lying. The jury found the youth pastor not guilty, and the judge let him go free. The young woman's reputation was tainted, and eventually she suffered a mental breakdown. It took Alice several years to recover and rebuild her life.

In each of these cases, and countless others, earthly justice eluded the victims. When there seems to be no recourse for an abuser's actions and the victim realizes we have a flawed human justice system, the capacity to trust can be further diminished. Life can feel hopeless, even meaningless. In such situations, the victim often grapples with the question, Will justice be done?

## JOSEPH'S STORY OF INJUSTICE

When I think about injustice, the story of Joseph in the Bible comes to mind. As the second youngest of twelve brothers and as his father's clear favorite, Joseph was deeply resented by his older siblings. They despised him so much that they plotted to kill him. But instead of taking his life, they seized the chance to sell him into slavery when the opportunity arose. At just seventeen years old, Joseph was ripped away from his home and sent to Egypt (Genesis 37:18–28).

The slave traders sold Joseph to Potiphar, the captain of Pharaoh's guard. But even with this tragic turn in Joseph's life, God's favor remained on Joseph. His hard work and integrity caught Potiphar's attention, and before long, Joseph was entrusted with the oversight of everything his master owned. Under Joseph's care, Potiphar's household began to thrive (Genesis 39:2–6).

Someone else noticed Joseph's success—and his handsome appearance. Potiphar's wife began trying to entice Joseph to have sex with her. Despite her constant advances, Joseph rebuffed her, telling her it would be a great sin against God and a betrayal of his master's trust (Genesis 39:8–9). Day after day, she tried to seduce him, but Joseph refused each time. Finally, she grew tired of his resistance. One day, when they were alone in the house, she grabbed him by his clothes, desperate to force him into submission. But Joseph, determined to honor God, managed to slip out of his cloak and run from the house (Genesis 39:10–12). Enraged, Potiphar's wife turned the tables, falsely accusing Joseph of the very thing she had tried to do—claiming he had raped her (Genesis 39:13–18).

Joseph was arrested and imprisoned for several years for something he didn't do. Once again, he was treated unjustly. Yet God remained faithful. He gave Joseph favor in the eyes of the prison warden, who eventually put Joseph in charge of all the other prisoners and the daily operations of the prison. Once again, God granted Joseph success in all that he did (Genesis 39:19–23).

Through an interesting series of events, God elevates Joseph from the depths of the prison to the heights of Pharaoh's palace. Through providence, Joseph found favor with the powerful Egyptian ruler, who ended up placing him in charge of the entire nation while he was just thirty years old. Joseph then marries an Egyptian wife, and they have two sons (Genesis 40–41). Life finally turns around for Joseph. He goes from being the teen who was trafficked by his brothers to the second most powerful person in all the land.

Then, just as Joseph had predicted, a severe famine struck Egypt and the surrounding countries. Thanks to God's guidance, Joseph had wisely prepared during Egypt's agriculturally prosperous years, storing enough food to feed those in Egypt and to sell to neighboring nations (Genesis 41:47–57). And who should come seeking food but Joseph's own brothers—the same brothers who had betrayed him years before (Genesis 42).

When they stood before their little brother, they didn't recognize him at all. Eventually, Joseph revealed his identity to them. Terrified that he would take revenge, his brothers begged for mercy. Instead of vengeance, Joseph showed them compassion. Three times he reassured them that God was the one who sent him to Egypt to preserve their lives and the lives of many others (Genesis 43–45).

Joseph understood that ultimate justice belongs to God. When his brothers asked for forgiveness, Joseph said, "Don't be afraid of me. Am I God, that I can punish you? You intended to harm me, but God intended it all for good. He brought me to this position so I could save the lives of many people" (Genesis 50:19–20 NLT).

Joseph knew what it meant to suffer trauma. He had been betrayed by his own brothers, trafficked to a foreign country, repeatedly sexually harassed by someone in power, falsely accused of a crime, and imprisoned without cause. He endured years of being overlooked by those who could have helped him. Yet, through it all, Joseph entrusted his life—and the injustice he suffered—to God's ultimate plan for good and God's perfect timing.

## WHAT ABOUT YOU?

The desire for justice is a natural response to experiencing sexual trauma. Victims of abuse are offered profound assurance in the Bible: the wrong done to you will not go unpunished. God is the righteous Judge, and he is passionately committed to justice.

Justice is a central theme in Scripture, reflecting God's very heart and character. His justice is not only perfect but also rooted in his holy and righteous nature. Deuteronomy 32:4 declares, "He is the Rock; his deeds are perfect. Everything he does is just and fair. He is a faithful God who does no wrong; how just and upright he is!" (NLT). This passage affirms that God's actions are always just and perfect, without a hint of injustice. And God doesn't merely promote justice; he *is* righteous, upright, just, and true.

Psalm 89:14 reinforces this truth: "Righteousness and justice are the foundation of Your throne; faithful love and truth go before You." This paints a powerful image of God's rule being established on twin virtues of righteousness and justice. Both are integral to his reign over all creation, and they reflect his unwavering commitment to do what is right.

God's justice is also deeply personal and filled with compassion toward those who have suffered injustice. His heart is tender toward those who have been wronged, particularly the oppressed and vulnerable. Psalm 9:9 offers us comfort with this promise: "The Lord is a refuge for the oppressed, a refuge in times of trouble." God sees your pain, and he is the strong refuge to which you can run.

Even when justice feels delayed or out of reach in this world, the Bible assures us that God will make things right. Time and again, Scripture demonstrates his dedication to justice for his people. The story of the Exodus provides a vivid example of this. When the Israelites cried out under their weight of slavery in Egypt, God saw their suffering and responded. In

Exodus 3:7–8, God tells Moses, "I have certainly seen the oppression of my people in Egypt. I have heard their cries of distress because of their harsh slave drivers. Yes, I am aware of their suffering. So I have come down to rescue them" (NLT). This powerful act of deliverance reveals that God is never indifferent to the suffering of his people—he always moves on their behalf.

## GOD'S ULTIMATE JUSTICE

The ultimate demonstration of God's justice is displayed in the person and work of Jesus Christ. On the cross, we see the great culmination of God's justice and mercy working in tandem. In Christ, God deals justly with sin while providing a way for sinners to be reconciled to him. Romans 3:25–26 captures this magnificently:

> For God presented Jesus as the sacrifice for sin. People are made right with God when they believe that Jesus sacrificed his life, shedding his blood. This sacrifice shows that God was being fair when he held back and did not punish those who sinned in times past, for he was looking ahead and including them in what he would do in this present time. God did this to demonstrate his righteousness, for he himself is fair and just, and he makes sinners right in his sight when they believe in Jesus (NLT).

In your search for justice, it's important to also desire that God's forgiveness be extended to your abuser. As difficult as that may be for you to do, God wants them to place their faith in Jesus so that they can be forgiven of their sins, including the horrific abuse that was done to you. God doesn't want anyone to perish, but everyone to come to repentance (2 Peter 3:9).

Consider what God says to the wicked in Ezekiel 33:11: "As surely as I live, says the Sovereign LORD, I take no pleasure in the death of wicked people. I only want them to turn from their wicked ways so they can live. Turn! Turn from your wickedness, O people of Israel! Why should you die?" (NLT). Note the emphatic tone and punctuation marks. God doesn't want the wicked to perish, but to find new life, eternal life in him.

## ETERNAL JUSTICE

After the sexual assault and murder of my daughter, I remember wanting to take justice into my own hands. Once my ex-boyfriend had been arrested, I envisioned going down to the police station and begging them to give me just five minutes alone with him and a baseball bat. I imagined exacting my own personal justice, playing that scene over and over in my mind. Oh, the heartache and pain that someone's heinous sin against you can bring! Who else can bear the weight of your agony if not Jesus? Ultimately, I knew my desire for vengeance was wrong and would only land me in a jail cell like his.

As those initial feelings faded, my heart softened a bit and I focused more on my grief and loss than on getting even. But then well-meaning friends would stir things up by making unhelpful comments like "You know what they do to child molesters in prison, don't you?" or "He'll get his, don't worry." As a Christian, those thoughts didn't sit well with me. His pain would not lessen my pain. And honestly, there was nothing anyone could do to undo this horrific tragedy and bring my daughter back (which is what I really wanted).

God began reminding me of his mercy and love—how he forgave all my sins freely because of Jesus's death on the cross. As I reflected on the truth of the gospel and how undeserving I was of Christ's mercy and grace, I desired mercy and grace to be extended to my daughter's offender. God also opened my eyes to the real enemy—Satan. He hated my daughter. He hates me, and he hates my ex-boyfriend. Satan's sole desire is to steal, kill, and destroy—robbing us of everything in this life, even life itself. But Jesus wants to give us life abundant and eternal (John 10:10).

As this truth settled into my heart, my thoughts shifted. Instead of wanting to see this man destroyed, I began to pray that he would come to know Christ. Now I envision a different future—a future where he, my daughter, myself, and countless others redeemed by Jesus are worshipping around his throne. That is the redemptive work only God can do, bringing sinners salvation, reconciling them to himself and to each other. What a glorious picture!

Those who refuse to place their faith in Jesus and continue in their sins will face the consequences of God's eternal justice in hell. Even if they escape punishment in this life, no one will evade God's judgment (John 5:28–29; Revelation 20:11–12). They will either accept Christ's atonement for their sins or bear God's vengeance in hell forever. Scripture makes this clear in Daniel 12:2, Mark 9:48, John 3:36, and Romans 2:2–8, which all point to the certainty of God's justice. Romans 12:19 urges us, "Dear friends, never take revenge. Leave that to the righteous anger of God. For the Scriptures say, 'I will take revenge; I will pay them back,' says the Lord" (NLT).

However, we must guard our hearts from rejoicing in someone's downfall. Proverbs 24:17–18 warns, "Don't rejoice when your enemies fall; don't be happy when they stumble. For the Lord will be displeased with you and will turn his anger away from them" (NLT). I'm grateful that the Lord hasn't left me with a desire for vengeance but instead led me to have Christ-like compassion for those who have sinned against me.

Two verses have helped me cultivate compassion for my offenders: Proverbs 5:22 says, "An evil man is held captive by his own sins; they are ropes that catch and hold him." And Psalm 116:3–4 says, "Death wrapped its ropes around me; and the terrors of the grave overtook me. I saw only trouble and sorrow. Then I called on the name of the Lord: 'Please, Lord, save me!'" (NLT). These Scriptures remind me of my own past—how I too was ensnared by the ropes of sin and death, trapped and strangled by their grip. I remember the weight of my sins—sexual immorality, abortion, and countless others like lying, unkind words, gossiping, and cheating. Sin suffocates our souls, and death has a stranglehold on every single one of us!

When I realized the death grip sin had on me, I cried out, "Jesus, I need you! Save me from my sin!" He set me free. I found freedom in Christ, and that's the same freedom I want for those who have sinned against me. However, this doesn't mean we shouldn't seek justice on earth. Because God is just, we can—and should—seek earthly justice when possible.

## SEEKING JUSTICE HERE AND NOW

I sat in the district attorney's office, and three years had passed since my ex-boyfriend's arrest. Everyone affected, including him, anxiously awaited his capital murder trial. Under Texas law, his offense allowed for only two options: the death penalty or a mandatory thirty-six years before parole eligibility. Life imprisonment wasn't an option at the time, but that's what I wanted for him. I no longer wanted him to die for what he had done. God had shown me so much mercy, and I felt the need to extend a measure of that mercy to him (Matthew 5:7). However, I had hoped that seeking justice would protect others from being harmed by him in the future.

Another year would go by before the trial began. I had lived four agonizing years without any closure. Justice had not yet been served, and I wasn't sure it ever would be, at least not in this life. Then, as the trial unfolded, I quickly learned just how flawed our justice system is for both victims and testifying witnesses.

Many victims of sexual abuse never see their day in court—often due to lack of concrete evidence. Sometimes all a victim has is their testimony. Today that often isn't enough. Personally, I think victims are frequently disbelieved because of the sinful nature of the human heart, rather than a lack of evidence. In some cases, victims provide physical proof like traces of semen or signs of trauma yet still face disbelief from a judge and jury. It's a tragic reflection of how our preconceived ideas can distort justice.

Often, this disbelief is masked as wanting to think the best of the accused. I've heard church leaders dismiss a victim's accusations by misquoting 1 Corinthians 13:7, saying, "Love believes all things." But if that's how they interpret this verse, why don't they believe the victim's testimony?

If you have not been believed—if you have even had Scripture twisted against you—I grieve with you. God grieves too over such a destructive misuse of his Word. Many church leaders and other Christians have drifted far from biblical law, which upholds the importance of a victim's testimony.

## CIVIL AUTHORITY AND THE CHURCH

Both the church and civil authorities have essential roles in delivering justice here and now. As the body of Christ, the church is called to be a voice for the voiceless and to stand against injustice. Micah 6:8 provides a clear mandate: "Mankind, He has told you what is good and what it is the LORD requires of you: to act justly, to love faithfulness, and to walk humbly with your God." When we are seeking to fulfill the requirement to "act justly" in the case of sexual abuse, we can learn much from Scripture in how to pursue earthly justice.

Biblical law stated that an accused person could only be found guilty if the facts were established by two or three witnesses (Deuteronomy 19:15; John 8:17; 2 Corinthians 13:1; 1 Timothy 5:19; Hebrews 10:28). Numbers 35:30 states, "No one may be put to death on the testimony of only one witness" (NLT). Yet there seems to be a contradiction to this law in

Deuteronomy 22:25–26. In this passage, we learn that in the case of rape, God makes an exception: "But if the man meets the engaged woman out in the country, and he rapes her, then *only the man* must die" (Deuteronomy 22:25 NLT, emphasis mine). Why this exception? Because the victim alone can testify to her experience if the perpetrator does not confess. A woman who is raped stands as the sole witness to her trauma, and God commands that she be believed, declaring her innocent.

Church leaders who become aware of abuse or assault must believe the victim's claims, report them to the appropriate civil authorities, and cooperate fully throughout the legal process. The church should embody God's heart for justice, creating a space where the needs of the oppressed and afflicted are met with compassion and action. Romans 13:1 reminds us, "Everyone must submit to the governing authorities, for there is no authority except from God, and those that exist are instituted by God."

If a church fails to pursue the proper legal channels when sexual abuse or assault is disclosed, particularly when the accused is a pastor, elder, or church leader, it inflicts great harm on the victim, the church, and the community at large. This negligence contradicts civil, moral, and biblical law, all of which reflect God's righteousness and justice.

Furthermore, a church that does its own internal investigation without involving civil authorities does much harm to all involved. What some may perceive as mercy for the perpetrator is, in fact, an evasion of God's justice. Ultimately, it is a tragic disservice to the victim, who needs protection and support (Proverbs 31:8–9), and to the perpetrator, who needs proper accountability (1 Thessalonians 5:14), civil and church discipline (Matthew 18:15–17; Romans 13:1–5), and to provide restitution to the victim (Numbers 5:5–7). By skirting the judicial system, the church violates Romans 13:2, which states, "So then, the one who resists the authority is opposing God's command, and those who oppose it will bring judgment on themselves." Be assured, even if a church sidesteps civil authority to avoid judgment for the offender, God's judgment will fall on the church. Justice will be done because God is just.

## ASSISTANCE FOR VICTIMS

In Deuteronomy 22:26, God's people were not only instructed to believe the victim, but they were also to make sure that the victim wasn't harmed. Verse 26 holds some vital instructions for the church, as well as incredible encouragement and empathy for victims, as it states, "Do nothing to the young woman; she has committed no crime worthy of death. She is as innocent as a murder victim" (NLT). Did you notice the Bible equates being raped to being murdered? My friend, God sees the depths of what sexual trauma has done to your soul. I hope you can see how deeply he desires to address what has happened to you.

According to Old Testament law, when a witness came forward to testify to a crime deserving the death penalty, which was death by stoning, the witness had to be the first to throw the stone. Then the entire community was required to join in, acting justly in delivering the punishment for the crime (Deuteronomy 17:7). This may seem barbaric or harsh to some, but it was a powerful method of keeping others in the community safe from similar harm at the hand of would-be perpetrators.

Local churches can and should be equipped to provide practical support and care for survivors of abuse and assault throughout the legal process and beyond. This includes emotional support, financial assistance, and helping survivors navigate legal and social services. Additionally, prayer is a powerful tool in the pursuit of justice. The church can and should pray for God's intervention, wisdom for all those involved in the judicial process, and advocacy and healing for victims. Due to sensitivity toward the victim and providing them with confidentiality, perhaps the ministry of prayer for the victim is kept to only those already in the know in leadership or a few trusted friends of the victim. If your church isn't willing to support you through this time of seeking justice, find one that will. Please know that even if God's people fail you, he never will (2 Thessalonians 3:3).

For some, healing from past abuse leads to advocacy. Once you've experienced God's healing, sharing your story—when you're ready—can raise awareness and inspire others to seek help. Engaging in community efforts, supporting protective legislation, or volunteering with organizations that assist survivors can transform your pain into a force for positive change. For now, focus on experiencing renewal through Christ and his Word.

## JUSTICE IN GOD'S TIMING

One of the most challenging aspects of seeking justice is learning to trust in God's timing. Ecclesiastes 3:1 reminds us, "For everything there is a season, a time for every activity under heaven" (NLT). Patience and trust in God's perfect timing are crucial as we navigate the complexities of seeking justice in a fallen world.

Though I waited four long years for the capital murder trial of the man who sexually assaulted and murdered my daughter, I look back and marvel at God's timing. During those years between her murder and the trial, God brought my husband into my life, along with much healing through his Word, both of which I needed in preparation for the trial once it did come. Had it happened any sooner, I wouldn't have been ready or had the loving support I needed to go through it. And God knew it.

As the defense attorneys tried to deflect blame from their client to others, attempting to drag my character through the mud, I stood firm on God's love, truth, and faithfulness. My identity was so secure in Jesus that none of their defense tactics fazed me. I knew the woman they portrayed to the judge and jury—a promiscuous woman who had committed murder herself by aborting her baby (and his)—was not the same person now being defamed on the stand.

Yet, the trial was incredibly difficult to endure. The hard physical evidence in the case was complex, even confusing, leaving the jury the difficult task of deciding guilt or innocence. Each day that I stepped into the courtroom and every night that I returned home brought new opportunities to surrender my heart and mind to the Lord, trusting his sovereignty no matter the outcome.

Amid the pain and uncertainty of seeking earthly justice, finding peace in God's sovereignty is essential.

Romans 8:28 comforts and assures us that "All things work together for the good of those who love God: those who are called according to His purpose." This doesn't mean that all things *are* good, but it does mean that God can and will bring good out of even the most painful circumstances.

On the final day of the trial, the jury deliberated for hours. When they had finally reached a decision and filed back into the courtroom, I reached for my husband's hand, offered up one last prayer to the Lord, and sat on the edge of my seat. "We find the defendant guilty as charged," announced the jury foreman. Tears streamed down my face as the judge declared, "All rise. The jury is dismissed." I watched each juror leave, one by one. Most of them looked at me and smiled, a few of them shedding tears of their own. After the last juror disappeared through the doorway, the assistant district attorney, who had prosecuted the case, turned to face me. I hugged him as tightly as I could, sobbing openly. "Thank you, thank you!" I exclaimed. But above all, my heart was filled with profound gratitude to the Lord.

Then came sentencing from the judge: "You will serve thirty-six years before you'll be eligible for parole." My ex-boyfriend would spend the majority of his life in prison. The world has changed a great deal since that day in April of 1996. He's missed out on so much. Meanwhile, I've enjoyed a rich and fulfilling life with a wonderful marriage, and my husband and I have raised three beautiful children. Though I have experienced other tragedies and forms of suffering since that time, my just, loving, gracious, and merciful God has been faithful to walk with me through it all. He will faithfully walk with you too if you ask him.

## A FINAL, FUTURE JUSTICE

The Bible speaks of a day when God will fully and finally execute justice. Revelation 21:4 offers a glimpse of this promise: "He will wipe away every tear from their eyes. Death will no longer exist; grief, crying, and pain will exist no longer, because the previous things have passed away." This vision assures us that all wrongs will be righted and that God's perfect justice will prevail. While we await the ultimate fulfillment of God's justice, we are called to seek justice here and now in our world today.

I sincerely pray that you will also see some measure of earthly justice after the suffering you have experienced. But above all, I pray you will trust God's good character and sovereignty, resting in his loving and faithful care. Only in his everlasting arms will you find lasting hope and peace as you endure your earthly struggles (Deuteronomy 33:27). Looking to the future, you can be confident that God will one day make all things right, wiping away every tear and ushering in his perfect, everlasting justice.

## FOR REFLECTION

1. If you have pursued earthly justice, what was the outcome, and how has it impacted your life?
2. How have you sought further help, especially if you haven't experienced justice on this side of heaven?

3. How have you been able to find lasting peace in God in the aftermath of your abuse, whether or not you received earthly justice? How has this impacted your view of God?
4. What encouraged you most in this chapter about God's eternal justice?

Read the following Scriptures and write out one or two truths that you can apply to your life regarding seeking God's justice here and now.

- Deuteronomy 7:9–11
- Psalm 145:8–9
- Proverbs 17:15
- Matthew 18:21–35

## FURTHER READING

- Garrett Kell, "Forgiveness," The Mentoring Project (podcast), 2025, https://thementoringproject.com/field-guides/forgiveness/.
- Jennifer Rothschild, *God Is Just Not Fair: Finding Hope When Life Doesn't Make Sense* (Zondervan Publishing, 2014).
- Nancy DeMoss Wolgemuth, *Heaven Rules: Take Courage. Take Comfort. Our God Is in Control* (Moody Publishers, 2022).

# Chapter 8

# AM I A VICTIM, SURVIVOR, OR SOMETHING MORE?

Labels—they can help, or they can hurt. On one hand, labels can be useful for organizing things, like your kitchen pantry or the tools in your garage. But when it comes to people, labels can be damaging. They can leave you feeling as though you've been permanently marked, branded by society in a way that's hard to shake.

Take, for example, the label "victim." We often hear phrases like "She is a victim of assault" or "He is a victim of abuse." Notice the word "is," which implies a state of being, suggesting that is their core identity. According to Merriam-Webster, a victim is defined as "one subjected to oppression, hardship, or mistreatment."[1] But should that define a person's identity?

Many who have experienced sexual trauma resist being labeled as "victims." It's a painful reminder of the helplessness they once felt and the trauma they endured. Instead, they often choose to rebrand themselves as "survivors," hoping to build a new identity after trauma—a way of seeking their own renewal. According to the Oxford Dictionary, a survivor is "a person who continues to live, especially despite being nearly killed or experiencing great danger or difficulty."[2]

"Survivor" sounds better—stronger. It's often used to distinguish oneself from others who have experienced sexual trauma. "Victim? Not me. I refuse to be called a victim. I'm a survivor." Do you see the rebranding of self, the reshaping of personal identity? Relabeling yourself can feel cathartic, like taking back control of something that was once beyond your control. It's a way to reassert power and redefine what happened to you.

If you've experienced sexual trauma—whether through mental or emotional manipulation, physical molestation, abuse, or assault—may I offer a better identity? It's the identity your Creator God gives to his people: "overcomer." The New Testament Greek Lexicon-KJV defines the Greek word for "overcome" as "to carry off the victory, to come off victorious."[3]

There's one requirement for adopting this new identity, and it's something that those who think of themselves as survivors may resist: To be an overcomer, you must place your full identity in God's Son, Jesus Christ. Why? Because Jesus is the only One who has completely conquered sin and overcome this broken world.

Jesus speaks directly to how we too can be overcomers in him. In John 16:33, he says, "'I have told you these things, so that in Me you may have [perfect] peace. In the world you have tribulation and distress and suffering, but be courageous [be confident, be undaunted, be filled with joy]; I have overcome the world.' [My conquest is accomplished, My victory abiding.]" (AMP).

Jesus, the ultimate Overcomer, gives his followers the power to overcome sin, death, and destruction—including trauma. First John 5:4 reminds us, "Whatever has been born of God conquers the world. This is the victory that has conquered the world: our faith." Furthermore, 1 John 5:5 teaches that faith makes you an overcomer: "And who is the one who conquers the world but the one who believes that Jesus is the Son of God?"

Do you have faith in Jesus Christ? Have you put your trust in him to pay for your sin? If so, you *are* an overcomer—not a victim, not a survivor. Overcomer is your *new* identity.

What if you aren't sure about all this Jesus stuff? Perhaps you simply picked up this book to help you deal with the past. It surely will *if* you look to the One who has overcome this world *and* its brokenness. You too can be an overcomer if you put your faith in Jesus.

## KEEP BEING RENEWED

Finding renewal after sexual trauma is not a one-time event but a recurring process. If you have a relationship with Jesus as the Lord and Savior of your life, you are no longer a victim or a survivor, but an overcomer! A Christian's life is one of constant renewal—continuously overcoming the power of sin and its effects on you. The theological term is "progressive sanctification"—a process in which we are continually being renewed and transformed to be more like Jesus. Sanctification is a key Christian doctrine that emphasizes our spiritual growth and transformation, which is initiated and sustained by God's grace. His means of grace for this growth include time spent in prayer, fellowship with other Christians, and the study and application of his Word—with the help of the Holy Spirit.

I wish I had better understood this as a young Christian. Unfortunately, like many new believers, I fell for the false notion that God somehow zaps you and makes you super-spiritual if you simply ask him. The problem with this untruth is that when struggles arise, you may find yourself questioning your faith, your identity, your salvation, and perhaps even God himself.

Once you come to know Jesus personally, he doesn't remove sin and suffering from your life. If he did, why would we need to continually be renewed? Why would he encourage us to be overcomers, conquerors? The Christian life is a fight.

Romans 12:21 says, "Do not be conquered by evil, but conquer evil with good." Every day we must battle evil: the evil in the world around us, our diabolical enemy the devil who tempts and seeks to destroy us, and the sin that remains within us—what the Bible calls our flesh, or sin nature. This ungodly trifecta—the world, Satan, and your flesh—wages war against your soul. As Christians, we become battle-weary, tired, and weakened by our daily skirmishes. That's why we need Jesus and the renewal he offers! We are not to be overcome by evil, but to overcome evil with good—the goodness of Christ. He works in us to change us to be more and more like him. That's how we conquer the evil that has been done to us; that's how we can truly overcome it.

Renewal after sexual trauma is rooted in this ongoing transformation (sanctification) as we depend on God's grace and believe his Word. Philippians 1:6

reassures us that "God, who began the good work within you, will continue his work until it is finally finished on the day when Christ Jesus returns" (NLT). This verse highlights the confidence we can have in God's faithfulness to continue his work in us, even when the path of renewal seems rocky and arduous.

In the context of healing from sexual trauma, sanctification involves the ongoing renewal of your heart, soul, mind, and strength. It is by these four facets of your being that you are called to love God above all else (Mark 12:30). Sexual trauma from abuse damages your heart, soul, mind, and strength. But since God commands us to love him with all of who we are, he commits to faithfully renew each of these four areas as we immerse ourselves in his Word, draw near to him through prayer, and gather with his people for growth and encouragement. By these gracious means, our perspectives and attitudes gradually transform us to be like Jesus, allowing us to experience true healing and freedom.

## FINDING RENEWAL WITHIN THE CHRISTIAN COMMUNITY

I remember the first time I shared my testimony at a church women's retreat. My goal was to minister the love and hope of Christ to the women gathered and encourage them that God can take something evil and use it for good. After I finished and sat back down, the microphone was opened to anyone who wanted to share.

For over two hours, woman after woman stood and spoke of the incredible pain and loss each had endured.

Many were survivors of sexual abuse and revealed they had never told anyone what had happened to them. Tears flowed, hugs were exchanged, and prayers were offered for one another. It was truly one of the most beautiful things I have ever witnessed.

The process of renewal is not meant to be done in isolation. God has designed the body of Christ to be a powerful source of support and encouragement. Hebrews 10:24–25 reminds us of the importance of living in community with other Christians: "Let us think of ways to motivate one another to acts of love and good works. And let us not neglect our meeting together, as some people do, but encourage one another, especially now that the day of his return is drawing near" (NLT).

Being part of a loving and supportive gospel-centered church provides a safe space to share your struggles, receive prayer, and grow in faith with other Christians. That doesn't mean you have to tell your entire church about being sexually traumatized. However, it does mean you are not alone because, statistically speaking, a large percentage of men and women in your local church have experienced sexual abuse or assault.

Your church likely has people who have endured and overcome the effects of sexual trauma and would cherish the opportunity to walk alongside you as you seek to overcome them too. Ask God to lead you to someone with whom you can share your story and who will understand your experience. Perhaps you can reach out to your pastor, a church leader, or a biblical counselor to ask if they know someone who has overcome sexual trauma and would be willing to talk with you. Don't go it alone. God wants you to find renewal from your past, and he often uses those he has previously helped to assist you (2 Corinthians 1:3–5).

## THE HOPE OF RENEWAL

Before you picked up this book, you may have thought there was no hope of renewal from the sexual trauma you've endured. Second Corinthians 4:16 holds a powerful truth about the hope of renewal we have in Christ: "That is why we never give up. Though our bodies are dying, our spirits are being renewed every day" (NLT). This passage speaks to the reality that while our physical and emotional scars may remind us of the trauma we've endured, they will one day be gone. Yet, in Christ, your inner self is continually being renewed by the Holy Spirit each day. This renewal is not dependent on your successes or failures but on God's unchanging character and promises.

The process of being renewed daily involves leaning into and relying on the truth of God's love, faithfulness, kindness, goodness, and grace. It means allowing his Word to reshape your understanding of your worth, identity, and purpose. Ephesians 4:22–24 encourages you to "throw off your old sinful nature and your former way of life, which is corrupted by lust and deception. Instead, *let the Spirit renew your thoughts and attitudes*. Put on your *new nature*, created to be like God—truly righteous and holy" (NLT, emphasis mine). As you embrace your new identity in Christ—as an overcomer—you will find the strength to move from living in the pain of the past to living with hope in him for your future.

## FOR REFLECTION

1. Reflect on your current journey of renewal and restoration. How can you more intentionally turn to Jesus for comfort and hope in your daily life?
2. In what areas of your life are you seeking joy and peace? How can trusting more fully in God help you experience these gifts of grace through the power of the Holy Spirit?

Read Romans 15:13 and write one or two ways that you can allow God's hope to impact your journey of renewal.

## FURTHER READING

- Nana A. Dolce, *You Are Redeemed: Devotions for Living a Whole New Life* (New Growth Press, 2025).
- Andrew Nicholls and Helen Thorne, *Real Change: Becoming More Like Jesus in Everyday Life*, ed. David Powlison (New Growth Press, 2018).
- David Powlison, *Making All Things New: Restoring Joy to the Sexually Broken* (Crossway, 2017).
- Paul David Tripp, *New Morning Mercies: A Daily Gospel Devotional* (Crossway, 2024).

# ENDNOTES

## Chapter 2

1. Henry, Matthew, *Genesis 34 Matthew Henry's Commentary*, Bible Hub, biblehub.com/commentaries/mhc/genesis/34.htm. Accessed 17 Aug. 2024.

2. Vera-Gray, Fiona, "The Impacts of Child Sexual Abuse," Centre of Expertise on Child Sexual Abuse, Child and Woman Abuse Studies Unit, London Metropolitan University, August 8, 2024, www.csacentre.org.uk/research-resources/key-messages/impacts-of-child-sexual-abuse/.

## Chapter 4

1. "Perpetrators of Sexual Violence: Statistics," RAINN, n.d., rainn.org/statistics/perpetrators-sexual-violence. Accessed August 17, 2024.

2. Neelam, Rasna Kaur, "Long Term Effects of Sexual Assault," Charlie Health, April 2, 2023, www.charliehealth.com/post/long-term-effects-of-sexual-assault.

3. "Cherpah—Old Testament Lexicon—KJV," Bible Study Tools, Salem Media Group, n.d., www.biblestudytools.com/lexicons/hebrew/kjv/cherpah.html. Accessed August 17, 2024.

4. "Bearing the Cross: Exploring the Unimaginable Suffering of Crucifixion," The Bible Says, Tough Topics Explained, June 12, 2024, thebiblesays.com/en/tough-topics/bearing-the-cross-exploring-the-unimaginable-suffering-of-crucifixion.

**Chapter 5**

1. "Naos Meaning—New Testament Greek Lexicon—KJV," Bible Study Tools, Salem Media Group, n.d., www.biblestudytools.com/lexicons/greek/kjv/naos.html. Accessed September 1, 2024.

**Chapter 6**

1. Munroe, Cat, and Martha Shumway, "Female-Perpetrated Sexual Violence: A Survey of Survivors of Female-Perpetrated Childhood Sexual Abuse and Adult Sexual Assault," *Journal of Interpersonal Violence*, U.S. National Library of Medicine, May 2022, pmc.ncbi.nlm.nih.gov/articles/PMC9901498/.

2. "Child Sexual Abuse Facts & Resources," The Children's Assessment Center, n.d., cachouston.org/prevention/child-sexual-abuse-facts/. Accessed August 18, 2024.

3. *The Pulpit Commentary* further explains the meaning of the word "abandoned," or "forsaken" in some translations, saying,

> The verb 'forsaken' is not in the perfect tense, as translated in the Authorized Version, but in the aorist; and it implies that during the three hours of darkness, Christ had been in silence enduring this utter desolation, which had now

> come to its climax. The Man Christ Jesus asked why he was thus deserted; his human heart would fain comprehend this phase of the propitiatory sufferings which he was undergoing. No answer came from the darkened heaven, but the cry was heard; the unspeakable sacrifice, a sacrifice necessary according to the Almighty's purpose, was accepted, and with his own blood he obtained eternal redemption for man.

*The Pulpit Commentary*, BibleSoft, Inc., 2010, at Bible Hub, https://biblehub.com/commentaries/pulpit/matthew/27.htm.

4. "Paratithemi Meaning—New Testament Greek Lexicon (NAS)," Bible Study Tools, Salem Media Group, n.d., www.biblestudytools.com/lexicons/greek/nas/paratithemi.html. Accessed Aug. 24, 2024.

**Chapter 8**

1. "Victim Definition & Meaning," *Merriam-Webster*, Merriam-Webster, www.merriam-webster.com/dictionary/victim. Accessed 29 Mar. 2025.

2. *Survivor Noun - Definition, Pictures, Pronunciation and Usage Notes | Oxford Advanced Learner's Dictionary at Oxfordlearnersdictionaries.Com*, www.oxfordlearnersdictionaries.com/us/definition/english/survivor. Accessed 30 Mar. 2025.

3. "Nikao Meaning - Greek Lexicon: New Testament (KJV)," *Bible Study Tools*, www.biblestudytools.com/lexicons/greek/kjv/nikao.html. Accessed 29 Mar. 2025.

## *MORE BY CAMILLE CATES*

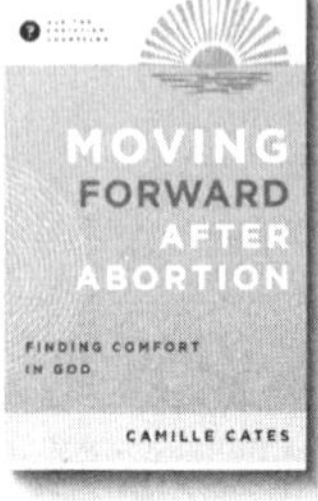


### MOVING FORWARD AFTER ABORTION

Even though each woman's story is different, the challenges that follow an abortion can be similar. Counselor Camille Cates helps women who may be facing hurt, confusion, and unanswered questions after an abortion find grace and mercy in God's love.

### PREGNANCY CRISIS

Faced with an unplanned or complicated pregnancy, you may feel overwhelmed or uncertain. Counselor Camille Cates offers hope, reminding you that God sees you, knows your circumstances, and offers wisdom, help, and love through Jesus—inviting you to trust his plan and walk this path with him.

## MORE FROM THE ASK THE CHRISTIAN COUNSELOR SERIES